DIMENSIONS
OF
RENUNCIATION IN ADVAITA VEDĀNTA

Dimensions of Renunciation in Advaita Vedānta

KAPIL N. TIWARI
M.A., Ph. D. (Phil.), Ph. D. (Reli.)
Senior Lecturer, Department of Religious Studies
Victoria University of Wellington

MOTILAL BANARSIDASS
Delhi :: Varanasi :: Patna

Indological Publishers & Booksellers,
Head Office : BUNGALOW ROAD, JAWAHAR NAGAR, DELHI-7
Branches : 1. CHOWK, VARANASI-1 (U.P.)
2. ASHOK RAJPATH. PATNA-4 (BIHAR)

First Edition : Delhi, 1977

PRINTED IN INDIA
BY SHANTILAL JAIN, AT SHRI JAINENDRA PRESS, A-45, PHASE-I, INDUSTRIAL AREA, NARAINA, NEW DELHI-28 AND PUBLISHED BY SUNDARLAL JAIN, FOR MOTILAL BANARSIDASS, BUNGALOW ROAD, JAWAHAR NAGAR, DELHI-7

To My

Revered Teacher

J.G. Arapura

PREFACE

The aim of this dissertation is to present a systematic exposition of renunciation (*Saṁnyāsa*) as a philosophico-religious category within Indian tradition with special reference to Advaita Vedānta of Śaṁkarācārya. This study dealing with the implications of renunciation in its personal and social dimensions is so all-embracing as to touch almost every popular spiritual conviction of the Indian mind and it overlaps almost every province of Indian philosophy. I have tried to justify this category as a spiritual technique systematically worked out and developed by Advaitins particularly Śaṁkara with a view to classifying and systematizing values in terms of the different forms which renunciation and its object may be found to assume. This dissertation also highlights not only lives of the enlightened persons but also principles of human behaviour in the Indian tradition implicitly clarifying thereby such concepts as *dharma* (socio-religious duties), the good life, obligation and responsibility etc.

In elucidating these concepts within the Advaitic ideal of renunciation, we are driven to conclude that this theory is not confined to the spiritual dimension of life representing the concept of *Mokṣa* (Release or Freedom) but is also the ground upon which a coherent and positive social philosophy can be raised. The attempt seems worth making in view of profound misunderstandings pertaining to the spirit of Indian philosophy in this respect especially Advaita Vedānta. The author believes that Advaita Vedānta, seemingly the most unworldly, is itself capable of generating social thought of a positive kind. The principle of renunciation is central to providing social order not irrelevant to such a task. This investigation seemed to me to be of special significance especially in the context of the present situation when renunciation has acquired an image of moral irresponsibility and hence has fallen into disrepute. To such critics I humbly give a Berkeleyian reply: "in such things we ought to think with the learned and speak with the vulgar.", and contrariwise — not quoting Berkeley —

we must avoid thinking with the vulgar but speak with the learned.

This effort is to think with the great *ācārya* (Śaṁkara) and some of his eminent followers with a view to clearing up misunderstandings about the matter prevailing among those who have not had the opportunity or even patience to examine the renunciation questions from the holistic perspective which those learned teachers have sought to inculcate.

For the debts I have incurred in completing this dissertation. I acknowledge my respectful gratitude to my supervisor, Professor J. G. Arapura who made me aware of the importance and positive aspect of this work. In spite of his extremely busy time, he read through the chapters of my dissertation submitted to him from time to time and helped me with his valuable suggestions and comments. It is impossible for me to adequately express my indebtedness to him whose judgments and encouragements will always remain a source of inspiration to this author.

Grateful acknowledgment is made to Professor T.R.V. Murti, ex-Professor of Indian Philosophy at McMaster University, for his valuable comments on some of the issues of this dissertation. Dr. K. Sivaraman read some of the chapters of my thesis and always encouraged me throughout the preparation of this manuscript. I gratefully acknowledge his help. Thanks are also due to Professor A. Shalom of the Philosophy Department for some of his critical reactions to an early draft of the present thesis.

I am thankful to McMaster University for offering me fellowship to conduct my research in the Department of Religious Sciences. My studies under Professor George Grant and Professor H. Mol were very stimulating and I should record my thanks to them. In the midst of preparing this manuscript, the author was given the opportunity to spend a year (1971-72) doing research in India where he came in contact with several Professors who helped him directly or indirectly. While it is impossible to list the names of all, he cannot fail to mention Professors N.K. Devaraja, A.L. Basham, D.D. Vadekar and R.K. Tripathi.

A more recent debt is to my distinguished colleague Professor Lloyd G. Geering, Head of the Department of Religious Studies at the Victoria University of Wellington, New Zealand. His help, advice and encouragement have always been a source of inspiration to this author.

VICTORIA UNIVERSITY OF
WELLINGTON, NEW ZEALAND

KAPIL N. TIWARI

CONTENTS

INTRODUCTION

NATURE, SCOPE AND LIMITATION

This study on the philosophico-religious category of Renunciation (in *Sanskrit-Saṁnyāsa*) in its personal and social dimensions grew out of my keen desire to dwell upon the essentials of Indian spirit and culture after previously studying some fundamental features of contemporary western philosophy, lying largely and perhaps significantly in the interested behavioural patterns of the individual and society. What I have in mind in the present dissertation is not "another" interpretation of Indian philosophical systems particularly the Advaita Vedānta but first and foremost a kind of reconstruction, the centrality and significance of which centre around the principle of Renunciation, giving rise to the personal dimension of life representing the concept of Freedom (*mokṣa*) but at the same time containing a background for a social philosophy, which we have called the social dimension of Renunciation. The attempt seems worth making in view of the divergencies that have marked the interpretations of the *Vedāntic* thought in this respect in our time.

Much has been written about the Advaita Vedānta of Śaṁkara but vast controversies still remain concerning the significance of Renunciation especially in its social sphere, for which we can hold none responsible except the subtle metaphysical structure of the philosophy of Advaita Vedānta itself as it is largely concerned with the problem of Ultimate Reality, i.e. *Nirguṇa Brahman* with its implied belief in the doctrines of *māyā* and *karma-saṁnyāsa* (action-renunciation) having its basis in *Jñāna* (metaphysical knowledge) for the realization of *Brahman.* It is on this account that Śaṁkara was criticized by a number of later thinkers for advocating the principle of *saṁnyāsa* (Renunciation) at the cost of the Hindu social structure based on the *karma-yoga* (action-theory) and *Puruṣārtha* (ultimate ends of life), which have their roots in the ideal of *lokasaṁgraha* (world-solidarity) throughout the Indian religious tradition.[1]

Whatever may be the central thrust of the Advaita Vedānta, an analysis and description of the religious trends of the society in which Śaṁkara formulated his thesis on Vedāntic lines and of his organization of the *maṭhas* (religious institutions) along with his extensive journeys throughout the country as the apostle of the *Vedānta*, preaching it not only among the elite but the masses, give strong indications of social relevance of his philosophy. In the present inquiry an effort is being made to show the possibilities of understanding not only the individual freedom but the meaning and function of society as well within the framework of Renunciation, fully taking into account the scepticism regarding its credibility.[2] But here it must be borne in mind that a justification of the social dimension of the Advaita Vedānta has to proceed along the lines of its metaphysical conviction with regard to Ultimate Being which makes everything else significant.

It is unfortunate that not much work has been done to explore the social dimension[3] of Śaṁkara's *Vedānta*, although there is no dearth of writing on the metaphysical aspect of it. The nature and characteristics of Renunciation in Advaita

1 Among the opponents, Rāmānuja, Dayānand Sarasvatī and B. G. Tilak could be mentioned. See K. Satchidananda Murty, *The Indian Spirit* (Waltair: Andhra University Press, 1965). Rahula Sankrityāyana and M. N. Roy who are apparently Marxists oppose Renunciation but to my mind, they have not themselves deviated much from the Hindu tradition. See M. N. Roy, *New Orientations* and also *Beyond Communism* (Calcutta: Renaissance Publishers, n.d.).

2 Many scholars find this attitude as "world and life-negating". See Albert Schweitzer, *Indian Thought and Its Development* (Bombay, 1960), S. J. Samartha, *The Hindu View of History, Classical and Modern* (Bangalore, 1959) and B. G. Gokhale, *Indian Thought Through the Ages: A Study of Some Dominant Concepts* (Bombay, 1961).

3 I believe that a positive world philosophy orientated towards a constructive action theory can be fully in accord with the *Vedāntic* metaphysics of *Brahman* and Freedom, perhaps in fact, be even drawn from it. In actual fact, we find the explanation of that potentiality has been achieved only exceptionally rather than in rule. The reason why the *Advaita* has not flourished as a common philosophy—the inadequacy of the *Vedānta* is partially right but to blame the theory itself is not justified.

To act positively on the basis of a positive ethics or philosophy of action would be easier for the generality of mankind than to base one's positive action on sheer freedom. To this extent the *Vedānta* may not have acted as a sufficient impulsion to accomplish all the positive things that we have come today to expect from philosophy.

Vedānta and the analysis of hypothesis involved in greater details, as brought out in the present inquiry, have made the author aware of its social aspect in harmony with Indian spiritual tradition.

The limitation of this study which it must be pointed out here, is that no attempt is made to present either a textual exposition or a systematic explanation of Śaṁkara's doctrine as such, or any part of the *Advaita* philosophy, although the Advaita Vedānta has been directly or indirectly taken to be the ground of consideration throughout. Rather an effort is being made to perceive the meaning of Renunciation implied in Indian philosophical writings, in modern terms.[1] The author is aware of the complexity of the problem and also of the danger he is exposed to in carrying the problem too far afield as that might result in some distortion of the teachings of the great *ācāryas*. In such matters, however, one is always to be guided by the maxims "Let Understanding be the Law", and "Life be the Goal".

There are ascetic trends in the Roman Catholic Monasticism and in the this-worldly Renunciation of Protestantism but they could not be brought into the purview of this study, although the author is aware of their importance. The reason for omitting them is the limitation of the scope of this undertaking as already indicated. The typologies of Renunciation outside the Indian spiritual world are extremely useful in understanding the present problem in general but they are so rather for a comparative study than for a work such as this which has express limitations. But the fact that the problem and its significance have been noted, and these could engross our attention for some later task. On the Buddhistic side, we could not achieve much either except the occasional references to it whenever and wherever they have been found relevant to the theme of the present work. The ascetic element in Jainism and its orientations to life in contradistinction to those of the 'Brāhmanic' and 'Buddhistic' is really a vast subject

1 It is noteworthy that most of the contemporary leaders who had great impact on Indian society directly or indirectly belonged to the ascetic tradition of the Advaita Vedānta. See Lloyd I. Rudolph and Susanne Hoeber Rudolph. *The Modernity of Tradition* (Chicago and London ; The University of Chicago Press, 1967), pp. 216-244.

and was, therefore, deliberately excluded, except partially, from the present undertaking in the hope of a future opportunity.

In defining and understanding the nature of Renunciation within its personal and social frameworks, the writer's purpose throughout is twofold. *Firstly*, I will investigate those passages of the *Prasthāna-traya* (the *Upaniṣads*, the *Bhagavad-Gītā* and the *Vedānta-sūtras*) which predominantly support the monistic doctrine of Śaṁkara with clear implications for *Saṁnyāsa*, which I have found, at the metaphysical level, identical with *Jñāna* and therefore realization of *Brahman*. There has also been a concern equally important to refute the claims of the ritualistic *Mīmāṁsā* (*Karma-Mīmāṁsā*) with which no compromise could be possible at the level of ultimate spiritual experience, viz. self-realization. It has been done with the Advaitic conviction, that, however important the doctrine of *karma* may be, which according to the ritualistic *Mīmāṁsakas* is the sole and central thesis of the Veda, it cannot explicate *Brahman* whose realization is the ultimate aim of the Advaita Vedānta. There is a dominant tendency on the part of Śaṁkara to lean more towards *darśana* (Philosophy) than *dharma* (Religion), not by abnegating the role of *dharma* but by making it subservient to the philosophical understanding of the structure of Reality.[1] The significance of this aspect of the problem has been thoroughly examined by presenting a detailed discussion on (a) *Various Motifs of Renunciation*, (b) *Typologies of Renunciation*, (c) *the Metaphysical Foundations of Renunciation* and (d) *the Personal Dimension of Renunciation.*

Secondly, I will examine the social dimension of Renunciation which has been worked out from the following points of view: (a) *the ultimate goal of Advaitic philosophy as representing a*

1 The sole task of *darśana* for the *Advaita* is understanding and realization of *Brahman* in its indeterminate form (*Nirguṇa Brahman*). But the goal that philosophy aims at cannot be accomplished without the religious means which in general represent the way in which we react to the ultimate problems of existence. These means must correspond to the result of self-realization. This correspondence between the philosophical goal and religious means cannot take place in a socio-ethical vacuum. Renunciation in the Advaita Vedānta is specifically a religious means which after accomplishing its spiritual task at the plane of *Jñāna* assumes a very positive nature and profoundly enriches the social dimension. It is important to extricate the Vedāntic method and understand its significance.

system of hopefulness. This is predominantly rooted in the Vedāntic structure of Reality in contradistinction to the nihilistic implications of Buddhism. To quote Professor M. Hiriyanna :

> The ascendency at one stage belonged conspicuously to Buddhism, and it seemed as if it had once for all gained the upper hand. But finally the *Vedānta* triumphed... The *Vedānta* may accordingly be taken to represent the consummation of Indian thought and in it we may truly look for the highest type of Indian ideal...On the practical side, the triumph of the *Vedānta* has meant the triumph of the positive ideal of life. This is shown not only by the social basis of the ethical discipline which the *Vedānta* as the orthodox doctrine commends but also by its conception of the highest good which consists...not in isolating the self from the environment as it does for heterodox schools but in overcoming the opposition between the two by identifying the interests of the self with those of the whole. Both ideals alike involve the cultivation of complete detachment; but the detachment in the case of the *Vedānta* is of a higher and finer type.[1]

(b) *The Institutionalization of Renunciation.* The highlight of this is the organization of the *Maṭha* (religious centre), *Pariṣad* (the group of Renunciants) and the *Saṁnyāsa* (Renunciation) for the guidance of mankind on the principles of love, fellowship and harmony. We will examine the roles of reformation *Saṁnyāsins* (Renunciants) within the framework of the social aspect of Renunciation.

(c) *The acceptance of the importance of the concepts of Īśvara (God), Deva (god), Avatāra (Incarnation) and Guru (spiritual teacher) for the purification of mind and the purity of conduct,* and

(d) *The recognition of the Varṇāśramadharma as various ingredients for the self-realization.*

Here what is important to note is that according to our interpretation, all these perspectives are fundamentally rooted in the structure of *Jñāna* towards the dawn of which they ultimately lead the seeker (the *sādhaka*) through the fulfilment

1 M. Hiriyanna, *Outlines of Indian Philosophy* (7th ed.; London: George Allen and Unwin Ltd., 1968), pp. 26-27.

of his obligations in a unique way, viz. renunciatory way. This point is of the greatest importance for the social life as it rests on controlling and overcoming anxieties and conflicts of life. The approach accounts for the pragmatic, humanistic and religious aspects of Indian philosophy. Some of the reformation movements within the social framework of Renunciation have also been discussed. These movements are more or less on the traditionalistic line of Śaṁkara himself who assigned a unified purpose to philosophy not by isolating it from the tradition but by directly confronting the tradition to make it a harmonious whole (*samyagadarśanam*) both at the individual and social levels.

As regards the question of the Indian tradition, we have found that Renunciation cannot be disposed of as a sporadic or random historical phenomenon. It is rather a continuous religious phenomenon which has throughout been subjected to serious appraisal to meet the spiritual need of the society. Whenever it has resulted in stagnancy, externalism or formalism, it has been re-examined and reformulated in order to provide the rigour and vitality to this principle. Renunciation was conceived and expounded by the *ācāryas* not only as a system to be posited but as a life to be lived. In this sense it serves the same purpose which philosophy serves in India. No doubt, the rationale of Renunciation has differed among parts of the Indian tradition but no system of thought in India could completely divorce itself from ascetic morality with the exception of the Cārvāka.

The Method

Methodologically, this work is descriptive as far as it represents the Advaitic tradition of Śaṁkara. A good deal of attention has been given to those trends of thought which exhibit a monistic tendency and an effort has been made to assess their significance within the Advaitic context of Renunciation. The assumption that modernity and tradition are radically contradictory rests on a misdiagnosis of the tradition. Our concern here is to accord priority to the tradition of Renunciation in the study of the Indian social structure and the problem of modernization by exploring the internal variations and hidden potentialities of Renunciation. The method is also evaluative with an emphasis on the practical aspect of Renunciation which has been inculcated until very recent times. If the reforms took place in Indian society, they were spontaneous, directly coming out of the spiritual experience of renunciants who are exemplary for the society.[1] The reformers of India have been spiritual leaders first and reformers later.[2]

Life and Work of Śaṁkara

In matters of historical nature often we have to work under severe limitation not knowing all the facts about Indian philosophers' life and their works. Philosophical writers in India avoid giving any details about themselves simply because they take it to be a futile task due to realization, in the words of Professor M. Hiriyanna, "that they grow from a soil that is ready-made for them and breathe an intellectual atmosphere which is not of their own making."[3] It was perhaps a result of a deep sense of egolessness and humility which they possessed. Śaṁkara's life is no exception to this fact. What can be said about it is conjectural but there are some evidences to establish the fact that he lived about 700 or 800 A.D. K. T. Telang attempted to place him in between the 6th and 7th Century A.D.[4] A. B. Keith thinks that Śaṁkara "may have been born in 788 and may have died or become a saṁnyāsin in 820 and at any rate, worked in c. 800 A.D."[5] According to the

1 *na me pārthā'sti kartavyaṁ triṣu lokeṣu kiṁcana /*
nānavāptamavāptavyaṁ varta eva ca karmaṇi //
(O Pārtha, there is left no duty in the three worlds for me; nor is there any not-acquired to acquire; yet, I am performing action.) *Bhagavad-Gītā*, chap. III, 22—(trans. mine).

2 "In the light of this it is easy to see why Gandhi was such a successful innovator, universally acceptable to India. For he first and foremost represented and achieved the 'ascetic' ideal and he united that with the *dharma* of politics so that it was felt that his politics was selfless and not directed to personal aggrandizement." S. J. Tambiah, "Buddhism and This-worldly Activity", *Modern Asian Studies*, 7, 1. (1973), p. 16.

3 Hiriyanna, *Indian Philosophy*, p. 14.

4 *Indian Antiquary*, XVI, (1887), p. 41f. Also see S.S. Sastri, *The Life and Teachings of Śaṅkarācārya* (3rd ed.; Madras: G. A. Natesan and Co., n.d.).

5 A. B. Keith, *History of Sanskrit Literature* (Delhi: Asia Publishing House, 1962), p. 148.

Āryavidyā-sudhākara:

> After this science of the highest spirit has suffered diminution through the sway of *Kali* age, it was supplied with a new force by the illustrious Śaṁkarācārya, in that he composed luminous and profound commentaries and the like of great compass to the *Brahmasūtras*, the *Upaniṣads* and the *Bhagavadgītā* and other scriptures which handed down the teaching of *Brahman*... The birth of Śaṁkara from the wife of Śivaguruśarman happened in the territory of Kerala in the Village of Kālaḍi after the 845th year of the end of *vikramārka* (*Vikramāditya*) had gone by.[1]

The above passage describes not only the life of Śaṁkara but also his mission to revive the Vedāntic spirit. The period in question is especially important because, on the one hand, of the dominance of several anti-Vedāntic systems, particularly Buddhism and also Jainism and on the other, the prevalence of various conflicting accounts of the *Brāhmanical* systems, making it very difficult to ascertain the real character of Indian philosophy. Professor S. Radhakrishnan summarizes Śaṁkara's life and personality as follows:

> The life of Śaṁkara makes a strong impression of contraries. He is a philosopher and a poet, a savant and a saint, a mystic and a religious reformer. Such diverse gifts did he possess that different images present themselves, if we try to recall his personality. One sees him in youth on fire with intellectual ambition, a stiff and intrepid debater; another regards him as a shrewd political genius, attempting to impress on the people a sense of unity; for a third, he is a calm philosopher engaged in the single effort to expose the contradiction of life and thought with an unmatched incisiveness; for a fourth, he is a mystic who declares that we are all greater than we know. There have been few minds more universal than him.[2]

1 See Paul Deussen, *The System of Vedānta*, Trans. Charles Johnston (Benares: Motilal Banarasi Dass, 1972), p. 36.

2 S. Radhakrishnan, *Indian Philosophy*, 2 Vols. (New York: The Macmillan Company; London: George Allen and Unwin Ltd., 1923) II. 450.

At a much earlier date Bādarāyaṇa in his *Vedānta-sūtras* and more recently Gauḍapāda in his *Māṇḍūkya-Kārikās* had drawn our attention to the monistic nature of the essence of Indian philosophy. Śaṁkara has paid his homage to Gauḍapāda whom he calls *paramaguru* (teacher's teacher). The most important contribution of Śaṁkara lies in his commentary (*bhāṣya*) on the *Vedānta-Sūtras* of Bādarāyaṇa wherein he establishes, with relentless logic, the doctrine of the *Vivartavāda* (the world as unreal manifestation of *Brahman*) but this doctrine, as we would see is not nihilistic or negative, contrary to common opinion. His commentary on the *Bhagavad-Gītā* provides an elaborate discussion on the principle of the *karma-saṁnyāsa* (Action-Renunciation) although it has been done with the acceptance of the efficacy of *karma-phala-tyāga* (Renunciation of the fruits of action or *niṣkāma karma-yoga*). It is well known that Śaṁkara also wrote extensive commentaries on the principal *Upaniṣads*, i.e., *Īśa*, *Śvetāśvatara*, *Kena*, *Praśna*, *Kaṭha*, *Muṇḍaka*, *Māṇḍūkya*, *Taittirīya*, *Aitareya*, *Chāndogya* and *Bṛhadāraṇyaka*.[1]

Some of the most popular works ascribed to Śaṁkara, in addition to these *bhāṣyas* are the *Upadeśasāhasrī*, the *Ātmabodha* and the *Viveka-cūḍāmaṇi*. Some popular hymns to the various forms of Godhead have also been attributed to him: *Dakṣiṇāmūrti Stotra*, *Harimīḍe Stotra*, *Ānandalaharī*, and *Saundaryalaharī*.[2] The last one has not been accepted as a work of Śaṁkara by Dr Belavalkar.[3] He thinks that some of the minor works like *Aparokṣānubhūti*, *Upadeśasāhasrī*, *Pañcīkaraṇaprakriyā* and *Śataślokī* have been written by Śaṁkara.[4]

Later Work on the Advaita Vedānta

Śaṁkara's Advaita Vedānta was further explained particularly with respect to the theme under consideration by his foremost disciple, Sureśvara, author of several works including *Naiṣkarmya-siddhi* which in substance propounds the theories

1 See Paul Deussen, *The Philosophy of the Upaniṣads* (New York: Dover Publications Inc., 1966), p. 29.

2 Radhakrishnan, *Indian Philosophy*, II, 450.

3 Sastri, *The Life and Teachings*, p. 25.

4 *Ibid.*, p.25.

of *Jñāna* and *Saṁnyāsa.* At a later stage, however, with respect to his metaphysical teaching, Śaṁkara's writings gave rise to two streams of interpretations, one represented by the *Vivaraṇa* school developed by Padmapāda in his *Pañcapādikā*, and the other represented by the *Bhāmatī* school of Vācaspati Miśra. In course of time, numerous books were written to explain the various aspects of the Advaita Vedānta. Some of them are: the *Brahmavidyābharaṇa* of Advaitānanda, the *Saṁkṣepa-śārīraka* of Sarvajñātman, the *Iṣṭa-siddhi* of Vimuktātman, the *Nyāya-makaranda* of Ānandabodha, the *Pañcadaśī* and the *Jīvan-mukti-viveka* of Vidyāraṇya, the *Siddhānta-leśa-saṁgraha* of Appaya Dīkṣita, the *Vedānta-paribhāṣā* of Dharma-rāja, the *Vedānta-sāra* of Sadānanda, the *Khaṇḍana-khaṇḍakhādya* of Śrīharṣa and the *Advaita-siddhi* of Madhusūdana Sarasvatī.

The Central Theme of the Advaita Vedānta

All of them agree with the central thesis of the Advaita Vedānta that *Brahman*, One's innermost Self, is the Ultimate Reality with which the individual Self is essentially identical. The Cosmos is located within this identity as being neither different nor indifferent but indescribable (*anirvacanīya*) from it. Any perception of difference or plurality in the Reality is attributed to *avidyā* (ignorance) which can be eliminated by *Jñāna* which goes hand in hand with *Saṁnyāsa* (Renunciation).

To know the non-dual Reality by identity with it is the end of the metaphysical quest. In fact, a fore-knowledge of it based on the scriptural texts (*Śruti*) and a fore-intuition are also the beginning of that quest, it being impossible under any other condition. Renunciation or *Saṁnyāsa* is thus both the extension into the realm of practical living, and at the same time the means to the realization (*Sādhanā*) of this already established identity. Thus Renunciation becomes the only valid way of living in harmony with the metaphysical identity of the individual Self with the Supreme *Brahman.* So far from robbing life of its values, it rather re-establishes them on a new foundation for spiritual life.

Renunciation as such cannot be defined independently by itself. Such an approach to Renunciation is not Advaitic.

This may very well be a key difference between the Advaitic standpoint and any other including perhaps, the Buddhistic. In fact, it is nothing of itself. It is to repeat what is said above, only an extension of knowledge into the realm of practical living. It is life being grasped by knowledge, leaving no other alternative. This is true of individual life as well as the life of society as a whole. At the same time it also acts as the only means to the realization of what has been given through theoretical fore-knowledge.[1]

1 For further details see J. G. Arapura, *Religion as Anxiety and Tranquillity* (The Hague, Paris: Mouton, 1972), pp. 100-107.

Chapter One

HISTORICAL BACKGROUND

Introduction

A LONG controversy, which still persists, concerns the origin and development of the idea and institution of Renunciation in India. The present chapter is an attempt to the understanding of Renunciation as a unique expression of the Indian spiritual consciousness. It is my contention here that *Saṁnyāsa*, which, is linked with asceticism and monastic organization, is the most fundamental trait of the Indian religious spirit which Indian philosophy and religion as a whole developed and hence is part of the whole of Indian culture. Asceticism was largely concerned with the man who sought spiritual realization, the *Sādhaka* (also described as *muni* or *yati* in the *Ṛgveda*), as he is called in the later technical language, his undertaking being directed to the quest for a direct contact with Reality or *anubhava* (spiritual experience). Monastic organization, on the other hand, was an aspect of institutional life of society. Bearing this in mind, it can be asserted here that Renunciation belongs to the common spirit of all Indian religions, including Buddhism and Jainism. Sureśvara, the foremost disciple of Śaṁkara, remarks that, though systems of thought including Buddhism may differ in their metaphysical orientations they are all unanimous on teaching Renunciation.[1]

The phenomenon of Renunciation in the whole of Indian tradition, is not based on the positivistic, anti-religious or anti-metaphysical outlook as might be the case with some of the ethical or humanistic traditions but it is an inseparable part of the *eschaton* of *Mokṣa* (Freedom) itself.[2] Since the understanding of the Ultimate reality and Freedom differs from system to system, the rationale of Renunciation is bound to differ and it

---

1 Sureśvara, *Vārtika on Śaṁkara's Bṛhadāraṇyakopaniṣadbhāṣya*, ed., K.S. Agase with Ānandagiri's *Śāstraprakāśikā* (Poona: Ānandaśrama Sanskrit Series, 16, 1892-94), pp. 513-15.

2 See, B. G. Tilak, *Gītā Rahasya*, trans. Bhalchandra Sitaram Suthankar (2nd ed.; Poona : Lokamanya Tilak Mandir, 1965), pp.665-714.

would be a grave injustice not to take into account the multi-dimensional nature of Renunciation. In fact, some scholars have interpreted this phenomenon without proper regard to this point. Indian philosophy, therefore, has resulted in simplifications, which are, moreover, inferred from a limited body of data. Conclusions based on such study need further revision and construction. Eleanor Roosevelt's following impressions of India state a widespread view :

> ...Prime Minister Nehru is trying to develop a democracy that, though perhaps not exactly like ours, will ensure all the people personal freedom. But if an accompanying material prosperity is also to be achieved—and the government will not be successful unless it can demonstrate certain progress on the material side—considerable education and re-education of the people will be necessary. For a belief in the virtue of renunciation is not an incentive to hard work for material gain; but only hard work by all the people is going to bring any real betterment of their living conditions. Somehow a spiritual incentive, a substitute for renunciation, will have to be found....My own feeling is that with their religious and cultural background something different will be required to spark in them the conviction that the modern struggle of a highly technologically developed state is worthwhile.[1]

Leaving the details of this remark to be considered in the following chapters, we may add here that the present survey of the growth and development of Renunciation throughout the Indian tradition and its various motifs show some of the peculiarities of the idea and the institution of Renunciation which refuse to be dogmatically classified into a rigid category of life-world negation.[2]

---

1 Eleanor Roosevelt, *India and the Awakening East* (New York : Harper and Brothers, 1953), pp. 196-202.

2 The bulk of research done by Milton Singer happily supports some of my convictions. See "Cultural values in India's Economic Development",—*The Annals of American Academy of Political and Social Sciences*, Vol. 305, (Agrarian Societies in Transition, 1956), pp. 81-91 : "Review of Max Weber's Religion of India", *American Anthropology*, LXIII, 1961 and "Religion and Social Change in India : The Max Weber's Thesis, Phase Three", *Economic Development and Cultural Change*, Vol. 14, 1965-66, pp. 497-505. Also see, Thomas R. Metcalf, *Modern India : An Interpretative Anthology* (London : The Macmillan Company, 1971), pp. 588-607.

Nature of Renunciation

It should be pointed out that the term 'Renunciation' (*Saṁnyāsa*) has different shades of meaning emphasized by different writers. Most of them have understood the term to mean isolation from, and indifference to the world. Commenting on the genesis of the Roman Catholic asceticism, J. L. Mackenzie points out : "The flight from the world was religiously motivated; it was an effort to achieve a closer communion with God by abandoning human society and human comforts."[1] A. J. Toynbee's observation on the Desert Hermits is as follows: "Turning their backs on the wickedness of the world, they sought redemption by the infliction of suffering on themselves."[2] Hence Renunciation has been taken to mean "the form of religious life led by those, who having separated themselves entirely from the world, live in solitude."[3]

In the Indian (*Vedānta*) tradition Renunciation has also been similarly defined. Thus while explaining the meaning of *Saṁnyāsa* according to Vidyāraṇya, the author of the great manual on Renunciation, the *Jīvan-Mukti-Viveka*, Pandit S.S. Sastri observes as follows :

> The path of liberation, according to Vidyāraṇya, is indicated in one word--Renunciation...Vidyāraṇya would not understand it in any but the formal orthodox sense in which the *Ṛṣis* of yore (Hindu Seers) principally employed it. Have no concern bodily or mental, direct or indirect, with the world, live in entire isolation, so to speak, and wear the orthodox insignia of the order—this is *Saṁnyāsa*, according to Vidyāraṇya.[4]

1 J.L. Mackenzie, *The Roman Catholic Church* (New York : Holt, Rinehart and Winston, 1969), p. 89.

2 Arnold J. Toynbee, "The Desert Hermits", *Horizon*, 12, 2 (Spring, 1970), p. 24.

3 F. Carnoy, "Monasticism", in James Hastings, ed., *Encyclopaedia of Religion and Ethics* (New York : Charles Scribner's Sons, 1915), VIII, 781.

4 Śrī Vidyāraṇya, *Jīvan-Mukti-Viveka* or *The Path to Liberation-in-This-Life*, eds. and trans. Pandit S. Subrahmanya Sastri and T. R. Srinivasa Ayyangar (Adyar, Madras : The Theosophical Publishing House, 1935), p. x.

The question, however, remains, how a life of entire isolation and indifference can ever be the end of existence, not to talk of Freedom? How can such a long tradition of Renunciation gain as much ground as it did throughout the Indian religious tradition on the basis of isolation? How can a Vedic religion, which Śaṁkara re-established, be possible on the sheer principle of indifference? Professor J.G. Arapura anticipates these while making the following statement : "Actually, the real reason for Śaṁkara's criticism of two systems, viz., the Sāṁkhya dualistic realism and Buddhistic subjective idealism (*Yogācāra*) is their inability to account for liberation. These may be singled out precisely because they are diametrically opposite and because their views, if adhered to, will destroy rational grounds of experience as well as the possibility of the world."[1] B. G. Tilak also refutes this theory of isolation as the central theme of *Vedānta* of Śaṁkara.[2]

In the light of the above observations, I am inclined to suggest that the pattern of Renunciation in the *Vedānta* has a different implication from what has been suggested by various scholars in terms of isolation or indifference.

> Two quite different conceptions mingle in the history of asceticism. One of these preserves the original meaning of discipline of the body for some ultimate purpose, as when William James urges sacrifice to God and duty as the means of training the will. The other conception distrusts the body altogether. Asceticism has then as its function not the training but the destroying of the body or the negation of its importance.[3]

What is especially noteworthy here is that the *Vedānta*, while agreeing with other systems pertaining to the significance of Renunciation, assigns a different reason for it. Early Buddhism

---

1 J.G. Arapura, "*Māyā* and the Discourse About *Brahman*", in M. Sprung, ed., *Two Truths in Buddhism and Vedānta* (Dordrecht, Holland : Reidel, 1973), p. 110.

2 "Buddhistic and Sāṁkhya asceticism is outside the purview of the Vedas and false; and as the path of Renunciation enunciated by me is consistent, with the Vedic religion it is true." (*Chān. Sāṁ. Bhā.* 2, 23, 1) Tilak, *Gītā Rahasya*, p. 764.

3 T.C. Hall, "Asceticism", in James Hastings, ed., *Encyclopaedia of Religion and Ethics* (Edinburgh : T. and T. Clark, 1909), II, 63.

might have succumbed to the temptation of unconditional and absolute Renunciation because of its different metaphysical outlook but the *Vedānta* would go against its nature if it sets up a doctrine of Renunciation independently of the *Brāhmanical* society and ethos from which it evolved. The objective of Renunciation is to provide opportunity for the progressive development of the various aspects of human personality with reference to which alone the social ideal can be attained. As M. Winternitz remarks: "It is in their opinion to be approached only from the point of view of the *āśrama* theory, according to which the *Āryan* has first to pass the state of *brahmacārin*, the student of the Veda, and of the householder (*gṛhapati*) who founds family, offers sacrifices and honours the *Brāhmaṇas*, before he is allowed to retire as a hermit or an ascetic."[1]

Here one might argue that the *āśrama* discipline was relaxed in later times as is the case with the Advaita Vedānta but it is to be remembered that even the *Vedānta* could not dispose of the importance of *brahmacarya* (student life) and perhaps the early Renunciation was a theoretical exception and not a general practice. A recent article of E. Skorpen in the *Philosophy East and West* states :

> But in Hinduism from greater antiquity another pattern of worldly withdrawal has also existed, quite different from the predominant Western or the Buddhist approach. This sprang from the Hindu conception of the four natural stages of life which after early childhood are those of student (*brahmacārin*), householder (*gṛhastha*), forest hermit (*vānaprastha*), and homeless mendicant (*saṁnyāsin*). On this pattern renunciation is the act not of people in religious communities who have not undergone secular experience and responsibility but of individuals who have—a difference of some note.[2]

Neither the West nor Buddhism offered the kind of scheme of life on the pattern of Hinduism as reflected in the *Brāhmanical āśramas* or in the *Paḍimās* of Jainism.

Taking into account the different emphasis we have laid on the nature of Renunciation, a working definition should be such

---

1 M. Winternitz, 'Ascetic Literature in Ancient India', *Calcutta University Review*, October (1923), p. 3.

2 Erling Skorpen, 'The Philosophy of Renunciation East and West', *Philosophy East and West*, July (1971), p. 284.

that it includes the motifs of various traditions and yet be relevant to the Indian context in general. In its most characteristic sense, renunciation would indicate a spiritual attitude having no superficial concern, direct or indirect, with the world as it forces itself mechanically and blindly upon us, for what characterizes the superficial structure of the world is its wrongness embodied in its relative and dependent status, too finite and too imperfect, to help achieve the tranquillity of mind, which once realized, transforms the nature of universe so radically (to the extent of its disappearance, as if) that the world becomes an arena for the discharge of motiveless activity at the religious plane, free from all anxieties born of egotism and self-aggrandizement. The present definition implies three elements : (a) renunciation aims at the denial and transcendence of the universe and the obligations associated with it only when the latter is approached independently of any Reality behind it. This is the world at its surface and therefore it does not attract the Indian spiritual thought which is based on reflection and self-culture. Hence the importance of *brahmacarya*. (b) The superficial structure of the universe is not denied dogmatically. Behind it is the strong support of *Śruti* (revelation), based on the understanding of each and every school which has its own cosmology, and (c) renunciation unfolds the meaning of existence by eliminating egoism (*ahaṁkāra*) which constitutes human conditioning and keeps oneself divided from the rest of the universe. It aims at the complete eradication of all obstacles, stemming from the gulf between the object and subject as if they were independent and autonomous.

These characteristics differ slightly in various traditions but the underlying theme of renunciation remains the same. It stands primarily for the self-culture which is essential for the social culture, finally culminating in the realization of the harmonious whole where all the conflicts completely disappear and the man becomes virtuous by nature.[1] But in order to justify the present standpoint with regard to the nature of

1. *Utpannātmaprabodhasya tvadveṣṭṛtvādayo guṇāḥ,*
ayatnato bhavantyasya na tu sādhanarūpiṇah. Naiṣkarmyasiddhi, IV. 69
"In a person of Self-Knowledge virtues like non-hatred establish themselves without any effort on his part. They are not of the nature of means to him. See Sri Sureśvarācārya, *Naiṣkarmyasiddhi*, Trans. S.S. Raghavachar (Mysore: University of Mysore, 1965) ; p. 172.

renunciation, let us turn to the Brāhmanical schools to ascertain as to what extent, this approach is plausible.

(a) *The Vedas*:

Without going into the controversy whether the Vedas represent a philosophy, system of philosophy, mythology or cosmogony, our aim is to see the elements of renunciation which the Vedic thinkers supplied for subsequent thought so much so that Indian philosophy could never cut itself off from the general structure of renunciation, tacitly implied or imperfectly conceived by the Vedas.

If the argument presented above is valid, it follows that in the Ṛgvedic times, the doctrine of renunciation was not unknown. There are also some evidences which prove that the Vedic thinkers also knew and promulgated the institutional aspect of renunciation, refusing the claims of those scholars who think that Buddhism actually introduced renunciation into Indian religions as it was absent in the Vedic thought.[1] It should be noted here that when the Buddha himself renounced the world, there are evidences to provide the existence of the renunciants as is seen in the "Legend of the Four Signs."[2] The legendary status of these signs might be disputed but the renunciation on the part of *Siddhārtha* cannot be regarded as original or without precedent.[3]

But the renunciation doctrine as we find in the *Ṛgveda* is markedly different from the one we find in the Buddhism in the sense that the former also incorporates such ideals as those

---

1. E. J. Thomas, *The Life of Buddha as Legend and History* (New York : Barnes and Nobles, 1927), pp. 58-59.

2. The four signs (*Nimittee*) are conceived in the Buddhist legends as guiding signs for the Renunciation of the Buddha. These are the sight of an old man, a sick man, a dead man and a wandering monk (*Bhikkhu*). The fourth one is significant in this connection although its scientific status has been doubted. However, the legends clearly show the presence of monk even before Buddhism was originated. See S. Dutt, *Buddhist Monks and Monasteries in India* (London: George Allen and Unwin Ltd., 1962), p. 36.

3. *Ibid.*, p. 36.

of *brahmacārin*[1], *gṛhapati*,[2] *muni* (ascetic)[3] and *Yati*[4] (*saṁnyāsin*).[5] The ascetics are called 'vātaraśanā'[6] (it stands for nakedness, "one having only the wind of air for one's waist-girdle.). The word '*Śramaṇa*' which became very favourite with Buddhism has been used in the *Taittirīya Āraṇyaka*[7] which belongs to the *Yajurveda*. The following remark of Professor G.S. Ghurye is very significant :

> The fact that in the *Taittirīya Āraṇyaka* (II, 7) *Ṛṣis* are said to have existed in former times, who were not described, as a little later they came to be, as either '*Saṁnyāsins*' or '*Parivrājakas*' but as '*śramaṇas*', that is those who were 'endeavouring', is significant. It should be noted that even in the *Bṛhadāraṇyakopaniṣad*, which cannot be much later than the *Taittirīya Āraṇyaka*, at one place (IV, 3,22), occur the terms '*Śramaṇa*' and '*Tāpasa*'. The passage in question describes the nature of the high stage of perfection.... Sāyanācārya explains the word *Śramaṇa* in this passage to mean Parivrājaka, ascetic, that is one who has entered the fourth of the four regular '*āśramas*'. He takes the term '*tāpas*' to stand for '*vānaprastha*', the third of the four '*āśramas*'.[8]

In the light of the above observation, the *Śramaṇa-Brāhmaṇa* controversy which denotes the two different systems of Buddhism and Brāhmanism loses its significance. The remark of Dr. D.R. Bhandarkar that *Śramaṇas* are non-Brāhmanic or non-Vedic also falls to the ground.[9] In the *Pātika*

1. *Ṛgveda*, X. 109.5. The word '*brahmacārin*' occurs only once in the *Ṛgveda*.
2. Cf. A.B. Keith, *The Religion and Philosophy of the Veda and Upanisads* Vol. I. (Delhi: Motilal Banarsidass, 1970), pp. 358-63.
3. '*Muni*' means one who meditates or reflects. In the *Ṛgveda* (X,136,2.) these '*munis*' are described as *vātaraśana keśin* (long haired, *Keśin*) and naked (*vātaraśana*), a sign of total renunciation. Indra is said "to be the friend of *munis*" *Ṛgveda*, VIII. 3.5.

   Munayo vātaraśanah bisanga vaste mala
   Vatasyānudhrājim yanti yad devāso avikṣatah. Ibid., X. 135. 2.
4. *Ṛgveda*, VIII. 3.9 and 6.18.
5. *Ibid.*, X. 72.7 "*Yad devā Yatayo yathā bhuvanānyabinavata*" (when, O ye gods, like *yatis*, ye caused all existing things to grow.) *Yati* has been explained in terms of the *saṁnyāsin*.
6. *Ibid.*, X. 136.2.
7. *Tai. Āra.*, 11.7.
8. G.S. Ghurye, *Indian Sādhus* (2nd ed.; Bombay: Popular Prakashan, 1964) p. 12.
9. D. R. Bhandarkar, *Some Aspects of Ancient Indian Culture* (Bombay, 1940), p. 53.

Sutta, the Buddha himself has mentioned *Śramaṇas* and *Brāhmaṇas* belonging to the Brāhmanical period. If *Śramaṇas* belonged to the pre-Buddhistic period including the Vedic period, it cannot be said that the ascetic order was the creation of Buddhism and references to the effect can be found in Buddhism itself.[1] Apart from *Śramaṇas*, even the '*yatis*' (meaning to control) constituted a separate class of ascetics who cherished independent views and did not believe in the Vedic ritualism. They belonged to the fourth *āśrama* of the *saṁnyāsa*.[2] Professor H.D. Sharma establishes the same fact :

> The *vātaraśana of the Ṛgveda*, who by the time of *Āranyakas* took the title of *Śramana* were the earliest dissenters from the orthodox Vedic religion. They are the same as the *yatis*....This *Śramana* is the *atyāśramin* of the *Śvetāśvataropaniṣad* (vi.21). Most probably it was before the rise of Buddhism that the old three *āśramas* were expanded into four....[3]

It is certainly true that a systematic exposition of either the theoretical structure of renunciation or the practical aspect of it, viz., *Āśrama* theory could not be legitimately expected in the Vedas, but in the background of the above discussion, it is clear that the Vedas themselves had some incipient ideas about the renunciation both in its individual setting as well as social or institutional.

Renunciation was introduced in the Vedas, unlike Buddhism, with reference to an *Āśrama* theory. Besides these references, we have clear indication of religious mendicancy as an institution of the Brāhmanical society in the *Bṛhadāraṇyaka*.[4] The view of S. Dutt that the institution of religious mendicancy was quite foreign to the Vedic *Āryan* society, signifying that it came from outside, namely, Buddhism, does not seem to be tenable.[5] The chief reason assigned by Dutt is that

1. *Dīgha-nikāya*, III. 28. "*Santi Bhaggava ek Samana-Brāhmaṇa Issarakuttaṁ Brahma-Kuttaṁ ācariyakaṁ aggannam pannapenti*".
2. Ghurye, *Indian Sadhus*, p. 17.
3. H.D. Sharma, "History of Brahmanical Asceticism", *Poona Orientalist* Vol. III, No. 4, (January, 1939), p. 43.
4. IV.3.22.
5. S. Dutt, *Early Buddhist Monachism* (Bombay : Asia Publishing House, 1960), pp. 60-63.

the '*yatis*' were not accepted as *Aryans* after discarding the sacrifices and Vedic rituals. But in our opinion, the *saṁnyāsa* as reflected in the lives of *yatis* is beyond all these superficial considerations and represents the peak of the spiritual life. Paul Deussen's following remark is very helpful : "Henceforth meditation alone is to serve as sacrificial cord and knowledge as the lock of hair, the timeless *Ātman* is to be both sacred thread and lock of hair for him who has renounced the world."[1] On account of this it is difficult to agree with Dutt who thinks that : "the Vedas contemplate man's life in one stage only, that of the pious and dutiful householder. The Vedas look to no beyond".[2] Professor B. Barua agreeing with the view of Rhys Davids remarks that :

> The Bhiksu order of homeless persons evolved originally from the *brahmacārins* (mentioned in the *Ṛgveda* once in X.109) who did not enter upon the stage of householders. .. the *śramanas*...broke away from past traditions, revolted against the older Vedic system of sacrifice and self-mortification or dissented from the later form of Brāhmanic religion....The revolt showed itself in every possible manner. For example, the *śramaṇas*... listened to nothing except their own conscience.[3]

The following conclusions may be arrived at regarding the position of renunciation in the Vedas:

(a) Contrary to the common belief that the Vedas do not entail the doctrine of renunciation, we have found that the Vedas provided incentives to the later development of Indian thought pertaining to the phenomenon of renunciation. In this sense the Vedas constitute the unbroken continuity of the tradition of renunciation.

(b) We also discovered that the renunciation as an institution is not the creation of Buddhism. It is an ideal which has a long history and can be discovered in the Vedas themselves.

(c) We also noted that renunciation does not take place in a socio-religious vacuum but it originates from life and cen-

1. Deussen, *The Philosophy of the Upaniṣads*, p. 124 ff.
2. Dutt, *Early Buddhist Monachism*, pp. 376-377.
3. B. M. Barua, *A History of Pre-Buddhistic Indian Philosophy* (1st ed.; Calcutta; Calcutta University Press, 1921), p. 242.

tres around life. Only the perspective into which it views life is different from that of the common morality.

(d) Another point which we indicated as a very important one was the prevalence of the four *Āśramas* in the Vedic times. It gave rise to the two streams of thought, one represented by the *smṛtis* dealing with the gradual progression towards the *Saṁnyāsa* and the other represented by the Advaita Vedānta that one may proceed from the state of *brahmacārin* to that of the *Saṁnyāsin*, and finally,

(e) By introducing the concepts of renunciation and *Jñāna* without systematically unfolding them, the Vedas provided guidelines for the future development of thought about Reality and renunciation for which alternative solutions were provided within and outside the tradition.

The evidences, however meagre, brought out so far from the Vedas show where the seeds of renunciation lay which eventually blossomed out in the *Upaniṣads*.

Although the Vedas are more oriented to this worldliness than the *upaniṣads* and the Advaita Vedānta of Śaṁkara, it is a fact that the general outlook of the Veda was accommodated with the Vedāntic spirit on the basis of the positive ideal of the former in which the Indian philosophy and religion were predominantly rooted. In this sense only the Vedas can be regarded as the source of all later thinking.

(d) *The Upaniṣads*[1]

In the previous section we noticed the implicit tendency of the Vedas towards linking renunciation with *Jñāna* and provid-

1. The word '*upaniṣad*' etymologically means 'sitting (*Sad*) nearby (*Upa*) devotedly (*ni*)'. 'The teachings of the *Upaniṣads* are regarded as a mystery (*rahasya*) for which only deserving candidates are qualified. The number of the *Upaniṣads* are over two hundred. However, those texts on which *Saṁkara* has commented are accepted generally as genuinely older ones and ascribed to the pre-Buddhistic period of 700-550 B.C. These *Upaniṣads* are also called *Śrutis*. See R.D. Ranade, *A Constructive Survey of Upanisadic Philosophy* (Poona : Oriental Book Agency, 1926), pp. 179-180. The thirteen principal ones of the *Muktika* Canon have been arranged in the following chronological order by the above author : *Bṛ Up.*, *Chān. Up.*, *Īśa Up.*, *Kena Up*, *Aita. Up.*, *Taitt. Up.*, *Kau. Up.*, *Kaṭha Up. Mun. Up.*, *Śve. Up.*, *Pra. Up.*, *Mai. Up.*, *Man. Up. Ibid.*, p. 13.

ing an institutional basis to renunciation. Because of a prominent place assigned to sacrifices and rituals in the Vedic scheme of life, the philosophy of renunciation which appeared strongly in the tradition could not be carried further. Because of the denial of ritualism and the Vedic sacrifices by the *Yatis* who constituted a group of renunciants, it would be correct to hold that exclusive emphasis laid on ritualism caused some confusions between religious and ritualistic values, giving rise to a trend in philosophy which shifted from the external and formal characteristics of ritualism to the inwardness of religious experience.[1] In my judgment, this constitutes the real significance of the upaniṣadic thought on the subject. They assign a somewhat different status to renunciation by relating it more closely with *Jñāna*, i.e. *Brahma-Jñāna* and yet without divorcing themselves from the tradition.[2]

There is a view of renunciation according to which it is a meditative act where contemplation plays a very vital role. Here the emphasis is purely inward rather than outward. The *Bṛhadāraṇyaka* gives a clear example of this. It attaches a different significance to the principle of the *Aśvamedhayajña* (the horse-sacrifice) and transforms it into a comtemplative form of renunciation, according to which everything is to be sacrificed for spiritual autonomy.[3] Here the universe takes the place of horse to be offered for spiritual progress and realization. The same *Upaniṣad* attaches a very positively interior orientation to what has been described as outward in the Veda: "Having become calm, subdued, quiet, patiently enduring and collected, one should see the Self in Self."[4] Commenting on the above

1. S. N. Dasgupta, *Hindu Mysticism* (New York : Federick Udgar Publishing Co., 1971), pp. 41-42.

2. George Thibaut, trans., *The Vedānta-Sūtras* (with the commentary by Śankarācārya) pt. I. (Delhi : Motilal Banarsidass, 1968), p. CIV "...most probably they are to be viewed not as creation of any individual mind, but as the gradual outcome of speculations carried by generations of Vedic theologians".

3. *Br. Up.* III 4, 1. See, Deussen, *The System of the Vedānta*, p. 8f.

4. *Ibid.*, IV. 4.23. "*Śānto dānta uparatas titikṣuḥ samāhito bhūtvātmanyevātmānam paśyati*". See S. Radhakrishnan, *The Principal Upanisads* (London : George Allen and Unwin Ltd., New York : Humanities Press Inc. 1969), p. 280.

passage, Paul Deussen remarks that the Vedic study, sacrifice, alms, penance, fasting are the more outward (*vāhya*) but tranquillity, self-restraint, renunciation, patience, concentration are the inward means to knowledge.[1] While emphasizing the role of renunciation as linked with Jñāna, the *Br. Up.* further asserts: "Men knowing *Brahman*, give up the desire for sons and wealth and prosperity and become almsmen".[2]

The above passages regard renunciation as a consequence of the *Brahma-Jñāna* as also a means of attaining it. These two positions brought out together in the *Upaniṣads* show the continuity of the Vedic tradition. As we would see that Śaṁkara's theory of *Karma-Saṁnyāsa* (action-renunciation), brought into line with *Jñāna* for its culmination in Self-knowledge has its basis in the Vedas. Renunciation, therefore, is not a negative act but the real culmination of the spiritual progress. There is no sense, therefore, in interpreting renunciation as something of a negative character.

It, therefore, becomes obviously an urgent matter to examine the question of renunciation as a religious attitude towards *vyāvahārika satya* (empirical truth) where the latter does not stand cancelled or negated but is transformed and transcended. This question can be examined theoretically from the standpoint of the Vedāntic analysis of Reality on the one hand, and by considering the role of the *Āśramas* (stages of life) at the institutional level, on the other. I submit that these questions are predominantly rooted in the Vedic tradition itself.

The fundamental doctrine of all the principal *Upaniṣads* is hard to discuss and decide here, but in the light of Śaṁkara's commentaries on the *Upaniṣads* and the *Vedānta-Sūtras*, there seems to be ground for believing that a diversity of opinion on this subject could not possibly arise.[3] This becomes more so because of the revealed nature of the *Upaniṣads* as a part of the Vedas in a literal sense. "Verily, this whole world is *Brahman*"

1. Deussen, *The System of the Vedānta*, p. 411.

2. Br. Up. III.5.1. "*etaṁ vai tam ātmānaṁ viditvā, brāhmaṇāḥ putraiṣaṇāyāś ca vittaiṣaṇāyāś ca lokaiṣaṇāyāś ca vyutthāya, atha bhikṣācaryaṃ caranti.*"

3. Thibaut, *The Vedānta Sūtras*, 1.1.4, pp. 22-46. See *Cha. Up.* VI,2,1, *Ait. Ara.* II. 4,1.1., *Br. Up.* II.5., 19 and *Mun. Up.*, II.2.11.

"... this my *Ātman* in my inmost heart is this *Brahman*".[1]

The understanding of this ultimate principle called *Brahman* and *Ātman* as the substratum or ground of Self and no-Self is based on the principle of Unity which renunciation unveils in terms of Jñāna. The *Mahāvākyas* "I am *Brahman*", "That thou art" can only be understood in key of renunciation which takes a very positive turn by isolating itself from everything other than the ground which is *Brahman.* But the isolation from everything else should not be taken in a negative sense as every thing is *Brahman.* Only in this context, *neti neti* (not this, not this) which describes the nature of *Brahman* helps the *Sādhaka* to reach the realms of *Īśvara,* known as *Saprapañca Brahman* (Cosmic *Brahman*) by transcending the limitations of the diversity of the Universe. This we have called the cosmic renunciation. If it is the ideal of God that is the central point of attention, the world of varieties and limitations will be transcended, as the existence of the world independently of God is inconceivable at the religious level of existence. The *Chāndogya* beautifully states : "Verily, this whole world is *Brahman,* from which he comes forth, without which he will be dissolved and in which he breathes. Tranquil one should meditate on it. Now verily, a person consists of purpose. According to the purpose a person has in this world, so does he become on departing hence. So let him frame for himself a purpose".[2] That is precisely the acosmic renunciation where God is replaced by the philosophic realization of God in terms of one's identity with the whole. The views as presented here are the same and if there is any difference, it is because of the differences in the standpoint from which the Absolute has been looked at. One of the *Upaniṣads* supports this contention: "To him he said: that which is the sound *Aum,* O Satyakāma, is verily the higher and the lower *Brahman.* Therefore, with this support alone does the wise man reach the one or the other."[3] Professor Haripad Chakraborti of Calcutta says:

1. *Chā. Up.* VIII.1.2. "*atha yad idam asmin brahma pure daharam puṇḍarīkaṁ veśma......tad vā va vijijñāsitavyaṁ*". See Radhakrishnan's note, *The Principal Upanisads*, p. 49.

2. *Cha. Up.*, III.14.3. *Maitri Up.* IV. 6. says '*brahma khalv idam vā va Sarvaṁ* : Radhakrishnan, *The Principal Upanisads*, p. 391.

3. *Pra. Up.*, V. 2 : '*etad vai, satyakāma paraṁ cāparaṁ ca brahma yad auṁkāraḥ tasmād vidvān etenaivāyatanenaikartaram anveti*'. See *Mun. Up.* 1.1.6

Śaṁkara draws our attention to the importance of *Saṁnyāsa* which may be said to be of two classes. One class is meant to be the means of true knowledge which every seeker aims at and the second class is resorted to by the man who has already had the vision of Truth and who desires to relish the blissful state of liberation even while living (*Jīvan-Mukti*).[1] These two types of renunciation are nothing but the cosmic and acosmic along with the cosmic and acosmic nature of Reality. The *advaitin's* insistence on renunciation stems from his metaphysics but his efforts to accommodate Vedic philosophy of action in its cosmic form is certainly of no mean significance. The discipline of *Karma-yoga*[2] is a step towards the acosmic renunciation. J.C. Oman observes :

> By the Hindu speculative theologians asceticism with a view to the repression of animal passions is regarded as means to the purification of mind, such purgation being an essential condition for the attainment of a complete knowledge of *Brahman* with its attendant freedom from *Saṁsāra*, i.e. embodied existence.[3]

The knowledge of the Supreme Reality, called *Brahman* and *Ātman* is conceived as the highest spiritual attainment and *Saṁnyāsa* is the key to unlock the door.[4] These *Saṁnyāsins* are known in the *Upaniṣdas* as 'knowers of *Brahman*'.

Renunciation in its Institutional Setting

Later *Upaniṣads*, referred to earlier, view the life of *Saṁnyāsa* as a kind of consummation to which man should progress. This position assigns a status to renunciation in the scheme of life (called *Āśramas*). It is a continuation of the implicitly conceived Vedic norm of life and therefore rooted in the Vedas. The *Chāndogya* mentions the first two stages, namely, the *brahmacārin* and *gṛhastha* and also speaks of *tāpas* as the third branch of duty and contrasts these three branches with the position of

1. Haripada Chakraborti, *Asceticism in Ancient India* (Calcutta : Punthi Pustak, 1973), p. 19.
2. *Mun. Up.* 2.2.8., *Br. Up.* IV.4.5.
3. J.C. Oman, *The Mystics, Ascetics and Saints of India* (London : T.F. Unwin, 1905), p. 9.
4. *Kaivalyopaniṣad*, 2——*na karmaṇā na prajayā dhanena tyāgenaikena amṛtatvaṁ ānaśuh.* (trans.—Not by work, not by offspring or wealth; only by Renunciation does one see the life eternal), Radhakrishnan, p. 927.

man who stands established in *Brahman*.[1] 'The passage names', says Paul Deussen, 'only three *āśramas*, recognizes their values, but contrasts with all three the "abiding steadfast in *Brahman*"; and this last is subsequently developed into the fourth *āśrama*'.[2] The fourth stage was exalted above the three *āsramas*, *atyāśramin*, as it is said in the *Śvetāśvatara*: "By the power of austerity and grace of God, the wise *Śvetāśvatara* in proper manner spoke about *Brahman*, the Supreme, the pure, to the advanced ascetics what is pleasing to the company of seers".[3] It is important to remember here that generally the stage of the *Paramahaṁsa* (the highest stage of the spiritual person, known as *Jīvan-mukta*) is not represented by men who may not have undergone the *Karmayoga* and its duties and responsibilities imposed by the Vedic culture. The *Dharmaśāstras* to which we come later highlight this development to which even the *Vedānta* is not an exception. The *Vedānta* with *Jñāna* carried its own social implications. The *Saṁnyāsa* is not formal or an external mode of living but an enlightened outlook. In fact, the several passages of the *Upaniṣads* confirm this. We hear of king Bṛhadratha who surrenders his kingdom, retires to the forest and gives himself up to the most painful mortification, gazing pointedly at the sun and standing with arms erect and yet he is obliged to confess—'I am not acquainted with the *Ātman*'.[4]

Considered accordingly, the Vedāntic Renunciation does not demand what is impossible and therefore the ascetic life was made an essential part of the brāhmanical religious system.[5] The dominant tendency of Indian religious thought still lies in the principle of *Jñāna-Karma-Samuccaya* (Union of Knowledge-Action theory)[6] and in my judgment even the Advaita

1. *Cha Up.*, II. 23.1.

2. Deussen, *The Philosophy of the Upaniṣads*, pp. 60-61.

3. *Śve. Up.*. VI. 21, Trans.—Radhakrishnan, *The Principal Upanisads*, p. 749.

4. *Mait. Up.*, I.2.

5. M. Winternitz, *History of Indian Literature*, trans. S. Ketkar (Calcutta : University of Calcutta, 1927), I.233.

6. Tilak, *Gītā-Rahasya*, p. 500.

Vedānta and the *Upaniṣads* do not appear to take an extreme view of denying the *Sādhanā* as instrumental to not only the socio-religious life but also for self-realization. Swami Madhavananda remarks :

> According to the *Vedānta*, there is no actual change in the Self, which is by nature pure and perfect. It is ignorance or *avidyā* that has covered its vision, so to say and it appears as limited and subject to change. Now this ignorance is embedded in the mind, and when the mind is thoroughly purified through *Sādhanā* or discipline the glory of the *Ātman* manifests itself.[1]

And here it must be noted the *āśrama* life embodies a system of vital social values, ethical principles, ends of life and ideals of conduct for structuring the life of society, founded on the *Āryan* tradition. The *Bṛhadāraṇyaka* asserts it : "On that path goes whoever knows *Brahman* and who has done holy works, as prescribed for the *āśramas* and obtains splendour."[2] While commenting on the *Śruti*, Śaṁkara makes it clear that the duties of *āśramas* are useful for the realization of Self.[3] The *Bhagavadgītā* characterizes the ideal of renunciation by exhortation to inculcate:

> humility, sincerity, non-violence, forbearance, simplicity, devotion to the teacher, cleanliness, perseverance, self-conquest, aversion to sense objects, freedom from egotism... equanimity in happiness and misery, devotion to God, love of solitude, pursuit of self-knowledge and the vigilant awareness of the final end.[4]

The *āśrama* like *dharma*, according to the *Vedānta* has a cosmic and a metacosmic aspect and these two aspects are closely inter-

---

1. Swami Madhavananda, trans., *Vivekachūdāmaṇi of Śankarācārya* (Calcutta : Advaita Ashrama, 1970), *Śloka*, 169, p. 65.

2. IV.4.9. *eṣa panthā brahmaṇā hānuvittaḥ tenaiti brahmavit puṇyakṛt taijasaś ca.*

3. Thibaut, *The Vedānta Sūtras*, Pt. II, III. 4.39 pp. 316-17. He quotes *Smṛti* 'Let a *Brāhmaṇa* stay not one day even outside the *āśrama*; having stayed outside for a year he goes to utter ruin.'

4. *Bhagavad-gītā*, XIII. 7-11. Cf. Swami Jagadananda, trans., *Upadeśasāhasrī of Sri Śaṁkarācārya* (Mylapore, Madras : Sri Ramakrishna Matha, 1961), 1-5.

linked as we shall see more fully later. N.K. Brahma's following remark is very pertinent to this point:

> Instead of denying that the *Vedānta* really describes a stage beyond the sphere of morality, we have to point out that as the Vedāntic experience, implying a transcendence of moral distinctions, comes after the severest moral discipline, which can, in no case be excused, but is regarded as essential and compulsory, it cannot justly be charged with ignoring or neglecting the development of moral side of our nature. The *Vedānta* only points out that there is something to be achieved even beyond the highest moral progress and reveals to us the nature of transcendent spiritual experience.[1]

Saṁnyāsa culminates in the transcendent spiritual experience according to which the world becomes a sacred world and the ideal of righteousness to which the *Saṁnyāsin* willingly corresponds is the ideal of God-man. *Saṁnyāsa* therefore is a sanctifying principle at the cosmic level and a sanctified principle at the metacosmic.[2]

The Various Motifs of Renunciation and Their Implication

1. *Tapas* (Austerity)

The word '*tapas*' etymologically means heat coming from the root '*tap*', to get heated. In the Vedic cosmology and cosmogony, it occurs in connection with the creative activity of Prajāpati.[3] There is another hymn which speaks of seven seers who attained a direct vision of truth by means of *tapas*.[4] Through '*tapas*', says another *Ṛgvedic* hymn, a poet (*kavi*) can see the old creations of the fathers.[5] In the *Atharvaveda*, *eka-*

1. N. K. Brahma, *Philosophy of Hindu Sādhanā* (London : Kegan Paul, Trench, Trubner and Co. Ltd., 1932), pp. 115-116.
2. *Chā. Up. Śāmkara bhāṣya*. II. 23.1. See G. N. Jha, trans., *The Chāndogya Upaniṣad : A Treatise on Vedānta Philosophy Translated into English with the commentary of Śaṅkara* (Poona: Oriental Book Agency, 1942), pp. 103-114.
3. *Tai. Āra.* speaks of Prajāpati's penance and its subsequent result. II.7 and also I.23.
4. *Deva etasyām-avadanta pūrve sapta Ṛṣayas tapase ye niṣeduh*
   bhimā jāyā brāhmaṇasyopanītā durdhām dadhāti parame vyoman.
   Ṛgveda, X. 109.4.
5. A. B. Keith, *Religion and Philosophy of the Veda and Upaniṣads*, pp. 210, 300, 437, 442-43.

vrātya as *Mahādeva* is said to have stood erect, for a whole year.[1] *Tapas* is a major theme of the *Brāhmaṇas* like *Śatapatha* and *Tāṇḍya.*

It is interesting to note that some of the *Upaniṣads* do accept the importance of *tapas* but mostly as a means to self-realization. The *Chāndogya-Upaniṣad*, for example, accepts *tapas* as an attempt for self-realization and assigns it a greater status than *Yajña* (sacrifice) which has also been accepted as equivalent to *tapas.*[2] Another *Upaniṣad* asserts that *Brāhmins* desired to know *Brahman* through austerity.[3] The *Kaṭha Upaniṣad* thinks that the knowers of *Brahman* (*brahmavids*) are qualified as '*Pañcāgnayaḥ*' (going round the five fires, a sign of austerity) and *triṇāciketaḥ* (keeping a rigorous *yājurvedic* vow).[4] Several other *Upaniṣads*[5] recognize the importance of *tapas* only as a technique of self-realization and strangely enough, nowhere it has been taken for the acquisition of occult powers which played a very dominant role in the Vedas.

The *tapas* in the pre-Upanisadic times was perhaps closer to the external mode of living and had therefore a limited bearing on the inward experience which became very central in the *Upaniṣads.* It is only on this line of thinking that we can appreciate the disbelief of Yājñavalkya in *tapas* in his preference of the *Jñāna* of *Brahman.*[6] Even the *Muṇḍaka Upaniṣad* rates tapas lower to *Jñāna.*[7] The *tāpasas* (ascetics who practised *tapas*) do not figure large in the *Jābāla Upaniṣad* either. The *Bhagvadgītā* does not favour severe austerity and insisted on the disinterested action as the true spiritual path :

> Though the religion of works...leads the devotee to the region of the Devas and the like, still, when practised in the spirit of complete devotion to the Lord and without regard to the (immediate) results, it conduces to the purity of mind (*Sattvaśuddhi*). The man whose mind is pure is competent to tread

1. *Atharvaveda,* XV, 1, 3, 3, 1.
2. *Cha. Up.*, II.23.
3. *Br. Up.*, IV, 4, 22.
4. *Kaṭha Up.*, 1, 3, 1.
5. *Mun. Up.*, I, 1, 8-9; I, 2, II; II, 1, 7, and II, 1, 5; II, 6; III, 1-5; *Śve. Up.*, VI, 21 and *Mai. Up.*, IV, 3.
6. *Br. Up.*, III, 8.10.
7. *Mun. Up.*, III, 2, 3-6.

the path of knowledge, and to him comes knowledge, and thus (indirectly) the religion of works forms also a means to the Supreme bliss.[1]

2. *Brahmacarya* (Celibacy)

Śaṁkarācārya while giving the advaitic exposition of the *Brahmasūtra* recommended *Jñāna* for Self-realization and reduced the exaggerated significance of austerity by incorporating it in the life of the *Brahmacārin*: "Him *Brāhmaṇas* seek to know by the study of the Veda, by sacrifice, by gifts, by penance, by fasting."[2] Similarly the following passage of the *Chāndogya* says that what people call sacrifice that is really *brahmacarya.* Sacrifice, Vedic studies, austerities etc. are means of knowledge and therefore belong to the stage of *Brahmacarya* (student life).[3] The *Kaṭha Upaniṣad* says: "That word, which all the Vedas record, which all penances proclaim, desiring which men live as religious students, that Word I tell thee briefly, it is OM.[4] The *Chāndogya Upaniṣad* mentions *Brahmacarya* as one of the pillars for righteousness and also a state that insures Brahma-realization.[5] Here it must be remembered that *Brahmacarya* was accepted not for a life of austerity but as a means to the acquisition of knowledge. The institution of *Naiṣṭhika Brahmacāri* (confirmed or life-long celibate) is fairly ancient, references to which are found in the *Bṛahadāraṇyaka.*[6] According to *Manu* "If he (the student) should like to live in the family of his preceptor for life, he should continue to serve him with diligence till he leaves his body."[7] In another passage of the *Chāndogya Upaniṣad*, sacrifice, the sacrificed, the '*Satrayana*' or relay of sacrifices, silence, austerity of fasting and retirement to forest are all one for one identified with the stage of *brahmacarya*; and it is declared that Self-realization brought about by *brahmacarya*

---

1. A. Mahadeva Sastri, trans., *The Bhagavad-gītā with the Commentary of Śri Śankarāchārya* (Madras: V. Ramaswamy Sastrulu and Sons, 1961), p. 6.
2. *Bṛ. Up.*, IV-4.22.
3. *Chān. Up.*, VIII, 5, 1.
4. *Kaṭha Up.*, I, 2, 15.
5. *Chān. Up.*, II. 23.1.
6. IV, 2, 1; 4, 22; III.5.
7. *Manu*, II.243.

is not perishable.[1] References should also be made to the *Kaṭha*, the *Praśna*, and the *Muṇḍaka* for the significance of *Brahmacarya*.[2]

While pointing out the significance of *brahmacarya*, Ghurye points out :

> '*Brahmacarya*', not only as an aspect of austerity but owing to its detachment from life, also as an opportunity for the persistent pursuit of knowledge, came to replace mere physical penance as a mode of spiritual endeavour. The need for moral qualities in this endeavour could not long remain Undiscovered....We therefore find the moral qualities of faith and truth given equal weight along with austerity, knowledge and *brahmacarya*.[3]

For the Advaita Vedānta, the state of *brahmacarya* was regarded essential for the cultivation of virtues, disciplines of mind and metaphysical knowledge, which if arisen due to the grace of the teacher would automatically culminate in the *Saṁnyāsa*. "Knowing this the people of old did not wish for offspring, what shall we do with offspring, they said we who have this Self and this world." and again : "But when all has become the Self of him, wherewith should he see another, wherewith he smell another."[4] In passing, it must be remarked here that the life of *brahmacarya* and the principle of austerity are found to exercise a positive action of the highest importance over the religious and moral nature of the individual although apparently they might give the impression of being systems of abstentions. Man's capacity to compel the environment and society depends upon the degree of his self-perfection, the extent to which he has purged himself of egotism, Self-interest and prepared himself by Self-discipline. He is always under constant self-appraisal and would not hesitate to retreat to fasting and other austerities to renew the purity which might give him new strength. A *brahmacārī* has tremendous confidence in himself which creates a phenomenon, called "*charisma*" which is based on the purity of life,

---

1. VIII, 5; 4, 3.
2. *Kaṭha Up.*, 1, 2, 15; *Praśna Up.*, 1, 9 and *Muṇḍaka*, III. 1, 5.
3. G. S. Ghurye, *Indian Sadhus*, pp. 25-26.
4. *Bṛ. Up.*, IV. 4.22; IV. 3.4; III. 9.26 and IV. 5.15.

constant vigilance and ceaseless application of his realization to the solution of the problem.

Brahmacarya here does not mean simply physical control. It means much more. An impure thought is breach of *brahmacarya* and so is self-deception. The *Manusmṛti* states : "But when one among all the organs slips away from control, thereby a man's wisdom slips away from him, even as the water flows through the one open foot of a water-carrier's skin".[1]

Śaṁkara was himself a "*naiṣṭhika brahmacāri*'. His revitalizing and organizing capacity was tremendous. In addition to enunciating the monistic philosophy, he created a vigorous revival and philosophical zeal among Hindu scholars. Morris Carstairs' recent findings on the implications of austerity support the present standpoint. By austerity and ritual control man can accumulate substantial life-force to controlling the environment.[2] Even traditional Hindu political thought exhibits the important tendency of inner control and principle of detachment for keeping the serenity of mind: "A king...who is voluptuous, partial and deceitful will be destroyed, even through the unjust punishments which he inflicts....Punishment cannot be inflicted justly by one...addicted to sensual pleasure."[3]

3. *Upavāsa* (Fasting)

Fasting generally means total abstinence from food and drink but usually it stands for light diet of restricted order. The *Taittirīya Saṁhitā* refers to three types of fasting, (a) living on food available in the village, (b) living on food available in the forest and (c) total fasting.[4]

It is interesting to note that some of the *Upaniṣads* and *smṛtis* assign a different meaning to fasting. The *Bṛhadāraṇyaka Upaniṣad*, for example, links fasting with *tapas* as a means to the Self-realization.[5] The *Mahābhārata* adds some more positive

1. Georg Buhler, *The Laws of Manu*, in F. Max Muller, ed., *The Sacred Books of the East* (Oxford : The Clarendon Press 1886), XXV, 48.
2. Morris Carstairs, *The Twice Born: A study of a Community of High Caste Hindus* (London, 1957), p. 86.
3. Georg Buhler, *The Laws of Manu*, p. 220.
4. P.V. Kane, *History of Dharmaśāstra*, 4 Vols. (Poona: Bhandarkar Oriental Research Institute 1930-53), IV, p. 52. Cf. *Tai. S.* I.6 7.3-4.
5. *Bṛ. Up.*, IV. 4.22. of Radhakrishnan, *The Principal Upaniṣads*, p. 279.

qualities for cultivation in the process of fasting which is not only *tapas* but also non-violence, truthfulness, freedom from cruelty, restraint and compassion.[1]

The Advaita Vedānta does accept the necessity of fasting for Self-purification but it does not go to the extreme of starvation. It is also quite strict regarding the type of food one should eat. The remark of Ghurye on fasting is worth noting :

> *Dasanāmis* observe the fasts of the 11th of the bright half of the lunar months of *Āṣāḍha* and *Kārtika* and the Krishna's 8th of the dark half of *Śrāvaṇa* as well as *Sivarātri*, the 14th of the dark half of the lunar month Māgha, as fasts. The first three are *Vaishnava* fasts and the fourth alone is *Śaiva*. *Anantacaturdasi*, the 14th of the bright half of *Śrāvaṇa*, *Dasara*, the 10th of the bright half of *Āsvin*, *Dipāvali*, the 15th of the dark half of *Kārtika*, and *Dattajayanti*, the 15th of the bright half of Phalgun are observed as festivals, as among the lay Hindus.[2]

Fasting is another characteristic of renunciation which is still prevalent in Indian society. It is usually meant for the purification of mind or imposition of expiatory suffering for the wrongs done by oneself. This kind of fasting might turn into a powerful kind called *dharnā* (a protest through fasting) at the house of the alleged oppressor and it is based on self-control and non-violent resistance. Even today in India, the best way of expressing protest is to abstain from meals.

Yajña (Sacrifice)

Among the various motifs of renunciation, sacrifice is one of the most difficult. In the Vedas a dominant place is assigned to sacrifices whose efficacy has never been doubted. It is regarded as a debt (*ṛṇa*) which constitutes the duty of every man towards gods and sages of old who preserved and transmitted the heritage of culture, towards the departed father and forefather (*Pitṛ*) and towards the guests and the race which is to be met by living a householder's life and begetting sons. The meaning or motive behind the sacrifice has been interpreted

1. *Śāntiparva*, 323, 17. Also Kane, *History of Dharmaśāstras*, IV, 54.
2. Ghurye, *Indian Sadhus*, p. 96.

differently occasionally. Its performance is taken necessarily for the material gain but, in fact, it could have the sense of discharging an obligation to the gods as is usually the case with the performance of sacrifice to *Prajāpati*, the creator par excellence. Secondly it might also serve the purpose of seeking the company of gods who are supposed to be present in Unmanifest form at the time of sacrifice. Thirdly, the performance of sacrifice also aims at the attainment of heaven (*svarga*), as pointed out by A.B. Keith : "the sacrifice is the ship which bears the sacrificer to that world....From another point of view the sacrificer mounts to the heaven : he does this by the special mode of recitation adopted."[1] Fourthly, the sacrificial performance also helps the seeker to live a life of truthfulness, Chastity, Self-restraint, fellowship and benevolence. It is based on a deep sense of shareability of what one possesses with others, including gods and departed souls.[2]

Whatever may be the shortcomings[3] of this type of ritualistic practice, it certainly serves a great role from the perspective of renunciation which got classified further in the Upaniṣadic time. It is based on the belief that there is a power or powers beyond the phenomenal world, resulting in the transcendence of the limitations of the phenomenal world on the part of the sacrificer. It also serves a very important religious function. It touches upon the relationship between man and gods—gods are not transcendentally or axiologically other from man but his friends and partners. This has a tremendous positive value for the growth and development of renunciation later.[4] Showing the positive and contributing aspect of ritualism in terms of renunciation, Professor M. Hiriyanna remarks:

> Even systems which do not first appear to countenance it are, as a little reflection will show, really favourable to it.

---

1. A. B. Keith, *Religions and Philosophy of the Veda and Upanisads*, II, 461.
2. *Kevalāgho bhavati kevalādī.* (He that eats by himself will keep his sin to himself). *Ṛgveda*, X. 11.6.
3. Some scholars think that too much of emphasis laid on sacrifices resulted in a sort of neglect of ethical ideas and gave rise to the practice of judging goodness by the standard of ritualistic correctness. For details see Hiriyanna, *Indian Philosophy* p. 46.
4. Some aspects of this problem have been discussed by Rudolph Roth in *Journal of the American Oriental Society*, Vol. iii, pp. 331-347. Also E. W. Hopkins, *Ethics of India* (New Haven, 1924), pp. 44, 61-62.

Thus ritualism with its promise of prosperity in a world to come actually results in complete Self-denial so far as this world is concerned, because the fruit of the deeds it prescribes is to be reaped not here, but elsewhere and amidst conditions totally different from those of the present life. The principle of detachment implicit in such doctrines was... rendered explicit, and even the ulterior motive of Self-love which is involved in striving for reward hereafter was eliminated by the *Gītā* with its teaching of disinterested action.[1]

It is undoubtedly true that the *Upaniṣads* tried to purge the sacrifices of their external and ritualistic significance but it would be wrong to say that they completely cut themselves off from the Brāhmanic tradition. Some of the *Upaniṣads* like *Bṛhadāraṇyaka*[2] and *Chāndogya*[3] depreciate the sacrifices and even condemn them but the normal view of the *Upaniṣads* is not quite against the performance of sacrifices. The sacrifice, however, is relegated to a secondary status which only helps man to reach the world of the Fathers, whence he would come back to the world after the exhaustion of his merit.[4] But some of the *Upaniṣads* assign some importance to the performance of sacrifices.[5]

The whole of the *smṛtis* more or less assign a role for the performance of sacrifices in the spiritual scheme of life. The attitude of Advaita Vedānta to this question appears to be one of synthesis. In fact, it cannot make a compromise with the sacrifice and renunciation at the *Pāramārthika* (Transcendental) level of spiritual experience but as regards the instrumental value of sacrifice for the dawn of gnosis and renunciation, it assigns it an inferior place along with other *Upaniṣads* referred to.

Jñāna (Metaphysical Knowledge)

By *Jñāna* in general we do not mean here the *vijñāna* (discursive knowledge) or *vṛtti* element of the internal organ which is the characteristic of *Jiva* (individual soul) as immanent in

1. Hiriyanna, *Indian Philosophy* p. 22.
2. iii. 9.6, 21.
3. i. 10-12; IV. 1-3.
4. *Ibid.*, V. 10.3; *Praśna Up.* 1.9; *Mun. Up.*, 1.2.10.
5. *Katha Up.*, 1.17; III. 2; *Mai. Up.* 1.1.

the *antaḥ-karaṇa* (internal organ or mind); the *vṛtti* element is relational and therefore contingent. As opposed to it, *Jñāna* is consciousness as such and therefore eternal, being intrinsically *Brahman* itself, which seems to be associated with empirical knowledge but is really untouched by it. All empirical knowledge is from its very nature directed to external things and therefore turned away from absolute consciousness and consequently manifests the latter as something different from what it is essentially. This process really accounts for the multiplicities and diversities of the world which constitute the source of anxieties, according to Advaita Vedānta. Renunciation as linked with the uncovering of *Jñāna* results in turning the concern of man away from external things to his essential inner nature by accomplishing which everything else is accomplished. *Jñāna* and renunciation take place simultaneously as one of the *Upaniṣads* says : "Verily, after they have found this soul, the *Brāhmaṇas* cease from desiring children, from desiring possessions, from desiring the world, and wander about as beggars".[1] Śaṁkara bases his whole philosophy on this foundation. He quotes the following texts to support the above contention : "The knower of *Brahman* attains freedom from all fear."[2] "When all desires occupying his heart, fall off entirely, then indeed, does the mortal become immortal."[3] Here it may be asserted that the monistic philosophy of Śaṁkara cannot justify its claim without ascertaining the role of *Jñāna* for the release from bondage which results from misapprehension, giving rise to attachment (*rāga*), aversion (*dveṣa*) and delusion (*moha*). Contrariwise, when misapprehension is destroyed by right knowledge, defects of existence are completely destroyed. This is followed by the destruction of attachment (*pravṛtti*) with the consequence of renunciation. The bondage that *Jñāna* and *Saṁnyāsa* are called upon to destroy is usually ascribed to Self's false association with the body, senses and the world etc. It is for this reason that Self-knowledge which leads

---

1. *Bṛ. Up.*, III.5.1; IV, 4, 22.
2. *Tai. Up.*, II.4:I. *Yato vāco nivartante, aprāpya manasā saha, ānandam brahmaṇo vidvān, na bibheti kadācana.* Also *Śvet. Up.*, III.8. (There is no way to salvation except through knowledge.)
3. *Bṛ. Up.*, IV. 4.7:, *Yadā sarve pramucyante kāmā ye'sya hṛdi śritāḥ atha martyo'mṛto bhavati, atra brahma samaśnute.*

to the destruction of *ahaṁkāra* (possible only on the basis of right knowledge and renunciation) has been rated to be of the highest value. This position has been established by denying any attributes to Self because if the attributes are real, they cannot be destroyed either by *Jñāna* or renunciation. For example, if agentship is real or natural to Self, it would make release impossible and so is the case with the question of suffering.[1]

Considered accordingly, what right knowledge and renunciation remove is the presentations and creations of *avidyā* (nescience) and not the real objects.[2] In other words, right knowledge and renunciation resolve not-self into the Self, and nothing but the Self or *Brahman* is real. Śaṁkara establishes his position not by positing *Brahman* against *Prakṛti* as the *Sāṁkhya-Yoga* does because in the latter case the aloofness and withdrawal of the Self from the not-Self will be real and categorically negative, but by positing the only reality of the Self and denying only the separate existence of the not-Self apart from Self which gives very positive significance to *Jñāna* and renunciation. *Jñāna* and renunciation in this sense are nothing but a positive feeling—if one may say so—of a vast expansion of the spiritual horizon which is essentially and eternally there, but in need of realization. It will be wrong to say that in the Advaita Vedānta, the not-Self is ignored and unfelt because no amount of reasoning can convince one of this. In fact, *Brahman* is the ground of everything and knowledge and renunciation simply unveil the nature of the ground which constitutes liberation.

For the *Advaitins*, *mokṣa* is not negative withdrawal from a real universe but is only correction of our vision of the nature of the world. Put simply, the *Vedānta* only spiritualizes the conception about the world and does not negate the world and therefore it should not be taken for the negation of the world but only for the transformation of the conception—the conception that *Brahman* is alone real and there is nothing within or without it as *Brahman* does not consist of parts and so far as this realization is lacking, the spiritual progress is in danger.

---

1. *Bṛ. Up.*, III. 7, 23: IV. 5.15; IV. 3, 21-32. For details see Thibaut, *The Vedānta Sūtras*, II, 2.3.40 and 2.2.10.
2. See S. S. Sastri and R. C. Kunhan, eds. and trans. *The Bhāmatī of Vācaspati: on Śaṅkara's Brahmasūtrabhāṣya* (Adyar: The Theosophical Publishing House 1933), pp. 134-40.

Here *Vedānta* makes an obvious advance over the *Sāṁkhya* which takes *Puruṣa* in isolation from *Prakṛti* which is real. Brahma observes :

> Hence if we thoroughly understand this Vedāntic conception of transcendence, we are not at all entitled to raise the question that so often seems to puzzle us, viz., what becomes of the world or of the body of *Jñānin*, after liberation is attained ? The answer is plain and the reason evident. Nothing happens to the world : the world remains what it was an eternal *anirvacanīya*; only the previous erroneous conception of it as real is now supplanted and corrected...[1]

In view of the Advaitins, the wholesale pessimism and negativism is by no means characteristic of renunciation. Pointing out the significance of the *Vedānta* for experience, the world and language, Professor J. G. Arapura points out :

> Actually the real reason for Śaṁkara's criticism of two systems, viz., the *Sāṁkhya* dualistic realism and Buddhist (*Yogācāra*) subjective idealism is their inability to account for liberation. These may be singled out precisely because they are diametrically opposite and because their views, if adhered to, will destroy rational grounds of experience as well as the possibility of a world.[2]

The *Vedānta* continues the Vedic tradition along its metaphysical lines, although the genius of the Advaita Vedānta is slightly different from the *Ṛgveda*. In the *Ṛgveda*, despite the fact that the renunciation doctrine has been recognized and explained, the *Jñāna* doctrine is not metaphysically linked with it. The *Vedānta* by accepting two truths reconciles some of the issues which the Vedic tradition posed before it. Professor M. Sprung suggests that :

> The Indians have two truths as a philosophical problem because they do not sunder faith and reason, but embrace all questions—including what in the West would be 'religious' questions—within the reach of philosophical thought. Hence religious experience and insight thrust forward the problem of two truths indefeasibly. In the West, because for the greater part we have held our religious faith to be of a different order than our philosophical convictions, we have had

1. Brahma, *Hindu Sādhanā*, p. 192.
2. Sprung, *The Problem of Two Truths in Buddhism and Vedānta*, p. 110.

little need to see things in terms of two truths : we are content with one truth and one faith.[1]

Without going into the further details of what Professor Sprung says, it could be safely said that at least for the *Vedānta*, the above statement is relevant. *Vedānta* exhibits a significant tendency of assessing the tradition and assigning it an adequate status. The *Saṁnyāsa*, for example is within the tradition as well as beyond it and so is *Brahman*.

Conclusion

In foregoing discussions, the central concern of the author, was to establish the following facts regarding renunciation: (a) Renunciation (*saṁnyāsa*) constitutes the essence of Indian philosophical and religious traditions and as such it is linked with *Jñāna* which is the sole means of Self-realization in the Vedāntic tradition. This aim has been gradually established by bringing out the *Jñāna* element as supplementary to *Karma* element. In this sense alone, *Śaṁkara* claims the supremacy of *Karma-Saṁnyāsa* over other means. The main purpose of renunciation along with that of *Jñāna* is a complete eradication of egoism which is absolutely necessary if man is to be free. This will only be possible when man has completely risen above his conditioned status.

(b) Moral and spiritual disciplines are to be cultivated in order to realize *Jñāna*. The emphasis has throughout been shown to lie in the inward experience that gives rise to the intuition of the metaphysical unity. This tendency might aim at transcending morality as commonly understood. Instead of trying to repel that change, I have tried to discuss the nature and scope of morality in the Indian scheme of spiritual life.

(c) Renunciation is not a negative ideal as it is primarily derived from a positive ideal of life. There are some traditions in which the phenomenon of renunciation has acquired a negative flavour but those traditions have always been re-evaluated in the light of the positive standard of the Indian mind and in my judgment they have not been very influential in Indian tradition. We have discussed some of the typologies of renunciation in the following chapter.

---

1. *Ibid.*, p. 5.

(d) We have also tried to examine the various motifs of renunciation and their implications for the understanding of human existence. What we have emphasized is that all these motifs represent various applications of renunciation. The cosmic and a-cosmic ideals of renunciation establish the same fact, i.e., the understanding of human existence in a spiritual context of life.

Chapter Two

TYPOLOGY OF RENUNCIATION

It will now be necessary for us to look into the typology of Renunciation in the Indian philosophical systems. So far we have largely been concerned with the nature of renunciation in the Vedas, the *Upaniṣads* and the *Brahma-Sūtras*. Of all the meanings that the word 'renunciation' assumes in those philosophical works, the most explicit is that which refers to the phenomenon of renunciation as a means of spiritual progress as well as the state of him who had the *Brahma-Jñāna*—the *Brahma-saṁstha*. The latter stage is, obviously, defined as an advance beyond the stages of life but it has also been noticed that even the *Vedānta* did not overlook the importance of *Sādhanā* (disciplines) and the socio-religious aspects of renunciation which have been linked with the tradition in general. The rationale of such a Vedāntic renunciation lies in its philosophical conception of Reality to which the religious implications of renunciation have been subordinated, may it be study, sacrifice, fasting, ritual, morality, *dharma* etc. The purpose of all this is to do away with the dispersion and automatism that characterize profane existence.

Nature and Importance of the Smṛti in the Context of Renunciation

The question we are confronted with in this section is the nature of renunciation which constitutes the subject matter of the *Smṛtis* or secondary scriptures. The word 'smṛti'[1] is very elastic and includes a variety of work such as the *Itihāsas*, the *Purāṇas*, the *Āgamas*, the *Darśanas* and popular literatures. It is impossible to discuss the doctrine of renunciation in all

1. "*Smṛtis* is a generic term applied to orthodox non-Vedic works in contradistinction to *Śrutis*, so that the *Dharma-śāstras* fall within the purview of *Smṛtis*. *Smṛtis* again is synonymous with *Dharma-śāstras* (*dharma-śāstram tu vai smṛtiḥ*)". S. C. Banerjee, *Dharma-Sūtras: A Study in their origin and Development* (Calcutta: Punthi-Pustak, 1962), pp. 4-5. These *Smṛtis* are also known as '*Smārta-sūtra*' '*Sāmayācārika-dharma*'. The precise meanings of these terms are debatable. *Ibid.*

these *smṛtis* but certainly disregard of the *Dharma-Śāstra* of Manu and the *Mahābhārata* whose compilation is attributed to Vyāsa and particularly the *Bhagavad-gītā* which forms the most important part of the *Mahābhārata,* will rather be inappropriate in such a treatise as the present one. This study will hopefully provide some guidelines for the forthcoming discussion on the social dimension of renunciation.

Here one point must be made clear. The tension between *Jñāna* and *Karma,* between the state of *brahmasaṁstha* and *dharma* has always been very forceful in every branch of the Vedāntic tradition. It defies any satisfactory solution. Although attempts have been made to establish a harmony between the two, the solutions provided in this direction are still open to controversies.[1] At any rate, the *Dharmaśāstras* and the *Gītā* have tried to deal with the problem very elaborately and perhaps their conclusions are of far-reaching significance. With the purpose of elucidating this problem further, we have presented a typology of renunciation taking also into account other religious systems such as Jainism, Buddhism and the *Ājīvakas.* Some of the religious sects within the Hindu tradition have also been briefly noticed simply because they presented a serious threat to the ideal of the Vedāntic renunciation.

"Hinduism, however, has always been mindful of the needs of all who have belonged to its fold", observes J. N. Farquhar, "and also the needs of the various sides of human nature, and it has not failed to provide practical guidance to man".[2] In the light of the above observation, we will examine these typologies irrespective of whether or not in the history of Indian philosophical thought, the above ideal has been reached. The

1. The very realization of righteousness leads one to an essential involvement in society and history. The Liberation, on the other hand, leads one in different direction—it is Being itself that is central point of attention. In the *Dharmaśāstras* and the *Gītā* a solution has been provided in terms of the socio-religious philosophy. The former concentrates on the *Varṇāśramadharma* and the latter on *Niṣkāmakarma* for the welfare of mankind. The common conclusions of the *Dharmaśāstras* however, based on values, in their attempt to link them with the concept of liberation, has not always been successful. The *Gītā,* on the other hand, by setting out to explain the metaphysical nature of Freedom has not been able to do the fuller justice to righteousness.

2. J. N. Farquhar and H.D. Griswal, *The Religious Quest of India* (London: Oxford University Press, 1922), p. 119.

Vedāntic thinkers are very clear on this point. Any endeavour lower than *Jñāna* and attendant on it *Saṁnyāsa*, cannot break the wheel of *Karma* although it may help the soul to achieve a state which can facilitate self-realization. It is on this account that the Vedāntic tradition in general has assigned a place to the *Pūrva-Mimāṁsā* as preparation of ground for the development of the *Uttara-Mīmāṁsā* (*Vedānta*), in which the ideals of *yajña* (ritual sacrifice) and *Svarga* (heaven) have been subordinated to those of *mokṣa* and *saṁnyāsa*.

A similar trend of thought will be noticed within the fold of the *smṛti* itself which has always been highly esteemed by most of the commentators of the *Vedānta*, including *Śaṁkara* himself, as is evident by their commentaries on the *Bhagvad-gītā*. This important shift of emphasis could never have been possible on a complete dissociation from the *dharma* which is rooted in the socio-religious philosophy arising out of the Vedas. Whether this transition is complete or incomplete will be examined later. The presence of such a fact is in itself very important especially in the face of allegations of other-worldliness against Indian philosophy. We noticed such a trend of thought earlier while dealing with the Vedas, the *Upaniṣads* and the *Brahmasūtras*.

Despite the fact that the *smṛtis* depend on the Vedas for their authority,[1] their overwhelming importance in the Indian tradition is undeniable. They have exercised a great influence on socio-religious life including the secular and political aspects (*Rāja-dharma* and *Vyavahāra dharma*).[2] Without going into the historical origin of these *smṛtis* which P. V. Kane proposes bet-

---

1. "Inasmuch as these *smṛtis* have emanated from human authors, and are not eternal like Vedas, their authority cannot be self-sufficient. The *smṛtis* of *Manu* and others are dependent upon the memory of their authors, and memory depends for its authority on the truthfulness of its source. Consequently the authority of not a single *smṛti* can be held to be self-sufficient like that of the Veda; and yet inasmuch as we find them accepted as authoritative by an unbroken line of respectable persons learned in the Veda, we cannot reject them as absolutely untrustworthy. *Tantravārtika*" see S. Radhakrishnan, *Religion and Society* (London : George Allen and Unwin, Ltd., 1969), p. 109f. cf. *Śāstradīpikā*, 1.3.4.

2. M. Winternitz's remark that the *smṛtis* are simply concerned with 'rules and regulations of duties of castes and the stages of life', obviously does not cover the all-comprehensive nature of the *smṛtis*. See Winternitz, *History of Indian Literature*, I, 275.

ween 300 and 100 B.C.[1], it will be correct to say that these treatises were written as supplements to the highly metaphysical conceptions of the *Upaniṣads*. It might be also assumed that the prevalence of Buddhism as anti-Brāhmanism must have attracted the authors of *Dharmaśāstras* to re-evaluate the Vedic tradition.[2] This task was found necessary not because of the long interval between the Vedas and the *smṛtis* but primarily due to the different emphasis laid on the central theme of the Veda by subsequent systems of thought, viz. *Vedānta* and the *Sāṁkhya*.[3] The emergence of some of the theistic schools such as the *Śaiva* and the *Bhāgavata* and of the epics the *Rāmāyaṇa* and the *Mahābhārata* also indicates a strongly felt need to supplement the rigorous monism of the *Upaniṣads* with its stress on *Jñāna* and *Saṁnyāsa*.[4]

But strangely enough, their treatment of the phenomenon of renunciation, shows the continuity of the syncretic nature of the Indian tradition, originating from the Vedas. The doctrine of renunciation in these treatises has been assigned a task to make the Vedic past serve the Hindu spirit in a way appropriate to the demands of socio-religious living. Due to the rise of the heretic schools, this was felt to be the most important. This adoption, however, certainly testifies to the tenacious continuity of the Vedic tradition. Only on this ground we propose to regard the renunciation of the *Dharmaśāstras* as being typologically different from renunciation in the *Upaniṣads*. The doctrine of renunciation in the *Upaniṣads* and the *Brahmasūtras* are fundamentally *gnoseological* in type whereas those in the *Dharmaśāstras* or *bhakti-śāstras* (devotional literatures) are socio-religious and devotional in type.

---

1. Kane, History of *Dharmaśāstras*, I, 59.

2. The age of the *Dharmaśāstras* is also known as the brāhmanical renaissance. It harks back to the Vedas which are regarded as the depository of the Āryan tradition. The greatest contribution of these treatises lies in their institutionalization of renunciation on the Vedic lines. This constitutes an important difference from the Buddhist concept of renunciation.

3. See K. Motawani, *Manu Dharma Śāstra* (Madras: Ganesh and Co. Private Ltd., 1958), p. 27.

4. R. C. Majumdar, H. C. Raychaudhari and K. Datta, *An Advanced History of India* (London: George Allen and Unwin Ltd., 1963), pp. 8, 403-404.

In the *Dharma-śāstras,* we find a detailed analysis of renunciation in innumerable places.[1] But the salient features of renunciation contain elements of vitality such as to contribute directly and effectively towards building a human social order. Gautama, for example, does not approve of direct entrance from the student life to the ascetic life and seems to favour the first three *āśramas* more than that of the fourth one.[2] The *Āpastamba* states that "he who lives in all these four according to the rules of law, without allowing himself to be disturbed by anything, attains salvation."[3] The *Yājñavalkya* prescribes rules for admission to the last two stages and thinks that only after the life of a householder the next two stages should be followed.[4] Manu believes in the gradual progression towards the *Saṁnyāsa. Mokṣa* according to Manu becomes the ultimate concern of man after he has undergone Vedic studies, procreated sons, performed sacrifices and cleared off all his debts to the sages, *pitṛs* and the gods.[5] Kauṭilya puts the householder's life at the top and forbids one to enter the order of asceticism without having discharged his duties to his family and society at large.[6] The *Yama*, *Śaṁkha* and *Likhita* also follow the principles laid down by Manu and Kauṭilya. There is a little doubt that the *dharmaśāstras* are unanimous in their preference of the stage of the householder. Asceticism has been accepted by all of them but they think that it should be entered after discharging one's obligations belonging to the first three stages of life.[7]

The task set by the *dharmaśāstras* is to produce a type of human personality that is dedicated to self-integration and a progressive social order; the standpoint adopted is both social and religious.

---

1. *Dharma-sūtra of Gautama,* III, 10-24. *Āpastamba-dharmasūtra,* II. 9.21. 7-20. *Baudhāyana-dharma-sūtra,* II. 6. 21-27, II.10. *Manusmṛti,* VI. 33-86. *Kūrmapurāṇa, uttarārdha,* ch. XXVIII. *Agnipurāṇa,* 161. See Kane, *History of Dharmaśāstra,* II-II. 930-970.
2. *Dharmasūtra of Gautama,* 3.1; 3.2.
3. *teṣu sarveṣu yathopadesam avyagre vartamānaḥ kṣemam gacchati. Āpastamba dharmasūtra* II.9.21-22.
4. *sūtra-vinyasta patnīkastayā vānugato vanam vānaprastho brahmacārī sāgnih sopāsano vrajet. Yājñavalkya* III. 45.
5. *āśramād-āśramam gatvā* (from one *āsrama* to another), *Manusmṛti,* VI. 34.
6. "*Kṛta-varnāśrama-sthitiḥ*", *Kauṭilya,* II.I.
7. S. Chattopadhyaya, *Social Life in Ancient India* (Calcutta, 1946), pp. 136-145.

In this sense it may be asserted here that, social morality in these treatises never emancipated itself from the religious goal of life, *Mokṣa*, for which *saṁnyāsa* was the highest and the final. This religious world-view, however, could not strictly be identified with the higher, philosophically oriented outlook of the *Vedānta*. This position can further be clarified by seeing their dominant tendency towards social standpoint over and above the *Jñāna* and *saṁnyāsa*—the latter, however dominated the Vedāntic philosophy.[1] But the general impression of the *dharmaśāstras* shows that the *gṛhastha* (householder) and *saṁnyāsa* were not at variance with each other but rather complementary. Sri Aurobindo sums up the above ideal :

> All these aspects of the *Dharma* were closely linked up together in progressive unity. Thus for example, each of the four orders had its own social function and ethics, but also an ideal rule and everyman by observing his Dharma and turning his actions Godwards could grow out of it into the spiritual freedom. But behind all *Dharma* and ethics was put, not only as a safeguard but as a light, a religious sanction, a reminder of the continuity of life and of man's long pilgrimage through many births, a reminder of the gods and plans beyond and of the Divine, and above it all the vision of a last stage of perfect comprehension and unity of divine transcendence.[2]

The difference between the Vedāntic renunciation and that of the renunciation in the *Dharmaśāstras* lies in the fact that, while for the former renunciation was the name given to the highest spiritual knowledge (*Brahmasaṁstha*) in the midst of intuitive experience and revelatory knowledge, for the latter, (and in this way similar to that of the Vedic thinking), it was taken to be one of the stages of life which must be attained after completing all obligations belonging to the first three stages of life. This was essential for the *Dharmaśāstras* in order to attain the prosperity (*abhyudaya*) as well as eternal happiness (*niḥśreyas*). The *Vedānta* accepts this contention and does not challenge their efficacy in helping the seeker towards the dawn of *Jñāna*. Only in this sense, we find a harmonious

1. N. K. Devaraja, *The Mind and Spirit of India* (Delhi: Motilal Banarasidass, 1967), pp. 140-142.
2. Sri Aurobindo, *Foundations of Indian Culture* (Pondichery: Aurobindo Ashrama, 1953), p. 190.

blending of the whole tradition in the *Vedānta.* According to the *Vedānta, dharma* associated with the various stages of life does purify the mind, and the knowledge of self is only manifested in such a mind.

On the whole, it seems that the second stage of life, i.e., *gṛhastha* was considered to be very important in the *dharmaśāstras* and the last one, namely *saṁnyāsa,* was taken to be the culmination of life where *mokṣa* is realized. For the *Vedānta,* on the other hand, the first state, i.e., the *brahmacarya* was regarded essential for the cultivation of virtues, discipline of mind, and for *Jñāna* and therefore essential for Freedom.

Renunciation in the Mahābhārata

The significant difference between the Vedic literature and the *Mahābhārata* lies in the fact that the ascetic practices in the former have not been directly related to social practices and institutions except casually, whereas in the *Mahābhārata,* the sense of disillusionment and detachment has been expressed with regard to the worldly activities but the fulfilment of obligations of various stages of life, has nevertheless, been recommended. In the *Śāntiparva,* Yudhiṣṭhira expresses his pessimistic sentiments even regarding the victory in the war: "Having caused the beloved son of Subhadrā, and the sons of Draupadī, to be killed, this victory that I have gained, is no better than defeat."[1] Yudhiṣṭhira's scepticism led him to contemplate renunciation but was however, held back by consideration of his duty as a warrior about which Nārada admonished him. Further it is interesting to note the following sentiments of Yudhiṣṭhira in favour of renunciation :

> Abandoning the pleasures and the conduct of uncultivated, practising rigorous penance, depending on fruits and roots for living I shall wander around in the company of animals in the forest...giving myself unconcerned with blame and praise, expecting nothing, attached to nothing, being above the conflicting emotions, without possessions...

---

1. *saubhadraṁ draupadeyāṅśca ghātayitvā sutān priyān,*
   jayo'yamajayākāro bhagavan pratibhāti me.

Śāntiparva, 1.15 R. C. Sastri Kinjawadekar, ed., *Śriman Mahābhārata* (Poona: Chitrashala Press, 1932), V, 2.

with a face ever cheerful and with senses thoroughly controlled.[1]

A sentiment similar to Yudhiṣṭhira's is expressed in the *Vālmiki Rāmāyaṇa* at the place where Sugrīva says : "Now, O Prince Rāma, I, the bearer of evil life, seeing the queen weep so bitterly and citizens crying in the agony of pain, feel a deep aversion towards the worldly pleasure"[2]

The sentiments expressed by Yudhiṣṭhira take a philosophical turn when *Jñāna* is given the supreme place in the scheme of asceticism as is evident from the following : "Through *tapas*, one attains the high, through understanding one reaches the height of excellence; the wise man, O Arjuna, achieves happiness through renunciation".[3] In the present passage we see the intermingling of the Vedic and Vedāntic trends of thought. The latter has been fully expounded in the *Mokṣadharma* section of the *Śāntiparva* but generally speaking, at no stage a total renunciation has been approved at the cost of obligations of the individual. The *Mokṣadharma* which represents here and there the tendency of 'other-worldliness' is not reconcilable with the general trends of the *Mahābhārata* but the co-existence of irreconcilables is not unusual in the *Mahābhārata*.[4]

The dejection we encounter in Yudhiṣṭhira in the *Śāntiparva* is similar to that of Arjuna in the *Bhagavad-gītā*: "O Kṛṣṇa, I don't want victory nor kingdom and pleasures. What for

---

1. *Caran bhaikṣyaṁ munirmuṇḍaḥ sapayisye kalevaraṁ*
   pānśubhiḥ samabhicchannaḥ śunyāgāravapratiśrayaḥ
   vṛkṣamūlaniketo vā tyaktasarvapriyāpriyaḥ
   na śocanna prahṛṣyanśca tulyānindātmasanstutiḥ, nirāśīrnirmamo
   bhūtvā nirdvandvo niṣparigrahaḥ. Śāntiparva, IX, 14-17. Ibid., p. 13.

2. *Yathāpratijñātamidaṁ narendra kṛtaṁ tvayā dṛṣṭaphalam ca karma*
   mamādya bhogeṣu narendraputra mano nivṛttam saha jivitena
   asyām mahisyām tu bhṛśam ruda tvam pure ca vikrośati dukkhatapte
   hate'graje saṁśayite'ṅgade ca na Rāmarājye remate mano me.
   Vālmiki Rāmāyaṇa IV. 24.4-5 See K. C. Sastrigal and V. H. Sastri, eds., *Śrimadvālmikirāmāyaṇa* (Mylapore, Madras : The M.L.J. Press, 1958), p. 457.

3. *tapasā mahadāpnoti buddhyā vai vindate mahat,*
   tyāgena śubhamāpnoti sadā Kaunteya tattvavit. Śāntiparva, XIX.26. See Kinjawadekar, *Mahābhārata*, V, 32.

4. Winternitz, *A History of Indian Literature*, I, 404.

kingdom or pleasure or even life."[1] Kṛṣṇa's exhortation to Arjuna for work reminds us of the *vanaparva* of the *Mahābhārata* where Draupadī disapproved of Yudhiṣṭhira's intention of total renunciation.[2] The teachings that actions must be performed in the light of one's religious duties which appear in the Tulādhāra-Jājala dialogue in the *Śāntiparva*,[3] the *Brahmin-Hunter* conversation in the *Vanaparva*[4] and the Kṛṣṇa-Arjuna dialogue in the *Gītā*[5] are not about action in the pragmatic sense. Actions are rooted in the religious structure of society. This ideal has been elaborately discussed in the *Gītā*. The real *tyāga* (renunciation) consists in not discarding actions but desire for the fruits of actions.[6]

The *Dharmaśāstras*, the *Mahābhārata* and the *Bhagavad-gītā*, it should be remembered here, are not isolated works preaching the philosophy of action as opposed to the ideal of renunciation. Their dominant tendencies exhibit the ideals they have in view, namely God-realization and the social-solidarity (*Loka-saṁgraha*). Both the ideals are fundamentally based on the principle of renunciation. God in the Hindu-tradition is not free from this *dharma* under which he himself works for the social-solidarity and the social-solidarity being based on the transcendental order, leads man beyond egoism and the idea of multiplicity. This attitude is fundamentally religious. It is based on the development of the Self which transcends its psycho-physical nature and works in the realm of ultimate meanings. The procedure by which these meanings are enacted in the *Vedāntic* and *Smṛti* traditions might slightly differ but

---

1. *na kāṅkṣe vijayam kṛṣṇa na ca rājyam sukhāni ca*
kiṁ no rājyena govinda kiṁ bhogairjīvitena vā.-Gītā, 1.32.
Tilak, *Gītā Rahasya*, p. 861.
2. *anarthāḥ sanśayāvasthā sidhyante muktasanśayāḥ*
dhīrā narāh karmaratā nanu nissanśayāh kvacit : *Vanaparva* 32.43 Kinjawadekar, *Mahābhārata*, II, 58.
3. *Śāntiparva*, 260-63, *Ibid.*, pp. 487-98.
4. *Vanaparva*, 206-215.
5. Tilak, *Gītā Rahasya*. III, 35, p. 934.
6. Hiriyanna remarks : "While it does not abandon activity, it provides the spirit of renunciation. It commends a strenuous life, and yet gives no room for the play of selfish impulses. Thus it discards neither ideal, but by combining them refines and ennobles both. That particular attitude of soul which renunciation signifies still remains; only it ceases to look askance at action. In other words the *Gītā* teaching stands not for renunciation of action but renunciation in action." Hiriyanna, *Indian Philosophy*, p. 121.

the goal is the same : preservation and transmission of a transcendent and universal order. Kṛṣṇa points out the same fact in the *Gitā* when he talks about the *Purātanaḥ Yogaḥ* (ancient Yoga) which is not an innovation as it has already been taught to Vivasvān who revealed it to Manu who transmitted it to Ikṣvāku.[1] The *Vedānta* establishes the same order in terms of *jñāna* and *saṁnyāsa* whereas the *smṛti* preserves the same tradition in term of *dharma*. Both the principles bridge the gulf between *saṁsāra* and *mokṣa*. Both of them alike do not snatch away the value of either individual or society or their interrelationship but transform them to such an extent that they become sacred. In such a religious phenomenon, the individual, society and the relationship between the two do not remain at the 'private' level but still preserve the identity, perhaps a better identity, by radically extending them at the level of the generality of mankind. This is perhaps the most revolutionary trait of the Indian tradition in general. The *Karṇaparva* of the *Mahābhārata* puts it—"The term '*dharma*' originates from the root '*dhṛ*', i.e., to hold or uphold and all human beings are held together by *dharma*. That by which the holding together takes place is *dharma*."[2] The ideal of *Brahman* represents the same truth, which virtually holds everything together as it is the Ground of everything. One of the *Upaniṣads* beautifully points out : "one who dwelling in the earth is distinct from the earth, whom the earth knows not, whose body the earth is, who rules the earth from within, he is thy soul, the inner guide, the immortal".[3]

Let us turn to some other types of renunciation in the Indian religious tradition to see more clearly their differences.

---

1. *imaṁ vivasvate yogaṁ proktavānahamavyayaṁ*
vivasvān manave prāha Manurikṣvākave'bravīt
sa evāyaṁ mayā te'dya yogaḥ proktaḥ purātanaḥ.
bhakto'si me sakhā ceti rahasyam hyetaduttamam. Bhagavad-gītā, IV.1-3.

2. *dhāranād dharmamityāhur dharmo dhārayate prajāh*
yat syād dhārana sanyuktam sa dharma iti niścitaḥ. Karṇaparva, 69.58. See Kinjawadekar, *Mahabharata*, IV, 128.

3. *Yah prthivyāṁ tiṣṭhan pṛthivyā antaraḥ yam*
prthivī na veda, yasya prthivī śarīraṁ, yaḥ
pṛthivīm antaro yamayati, eṣa ta ātmāntaryāmy amṛtaḥ. Bṛ. Up. III.7.3, Radhakrishnan, *The Principal Upanisads*, p. 225.

Renunciation in Jainism

We need not embark upon the history of renunciation in Jainism. To do so would be to go far beyond the scope of the present undertaking. But it is important to show the salient features of renunciation in Jainism in order to see more clearly its differences from those of Buddhism, *Ājīvikism* and the *Vedānta*. It is curious to note that though the Jainism is a religious system parallel to Buddhism, independent of *Brāhmanism*, it resembles both in several respects, particularly in the matter of renunciation. It is on this account that scholars like E. W. Hopkins regard it as "a theological mean between *Brāhmanism* and Buddhism."[1] Whatever may be the controversy over this question, it is a fact that renunciation in Jainism has certainly been influenced by the Brāhmanic tradition and has in itself exercised a great influence on at least early Buddhism.[2] Pointing out the importance of this historical phenomenon, H. Jacobi remarks: "The records of the Buddhists and Jainas about the Philosophical ideas current at the time of the Buddha and Mahāvīra, meagre though they may be, are of the greatest importance to the historian of the epoch. For they show us the ground on which, and the materials with which a religious reformer had to build up his system".[3] The philosophical and religious speculations of Jainism pertaining to the nature of renunciation is of a special interest to us because it helped the later Vedāntic thinkers correct some of the shortcomings into which these anti-Brāhmanical systems had fallen. In addition to Jainism and Buddhism, some of the anti-Vedic and anti-brāhmanic teachers who prevailed during that time are: Purāṇa Kassapa, Mākkhali Gosāla, Ajita Kesa-Kambala, Pakuḍha-Kaccāyana and Sanjaya Belaṭṭhaputta.[4] The general religious atmosphere of the time predominantly con-

1. Hopkins. *Religions of India*, p. 283.

2. For some aspects of this problem see H. Jacobi *Jain Sūtras*, in F. Max Muller, ed; *Sacred Books of the East* (Oxford: The Clarendon Press, 1884), XXII, Introduction.

3. *Ibid.*, p. XXVII.

4. Benimadhava Barua, *A History of Pre-Buddhistic Philosophy* (2nd ed.; Delhi : Motilal Banarsidass, 1970), p. 189.

sisted of the ascetic life or the life of hermits and wanderers. T. W. Rhys Davids points out :

> In the forests adjoining the settlements the disciples of the various schools, living a hermit life, occupied themselves, according to the various tendencies of the schools to which they belonged, either in meditation or in sacrificial rites, or in practices of self-torture, or in repeating over themselves, and teaching to their pupils, the *Sūttas* containing the tenets of their school. Much time was spent in gathering fruits and roots for their sustenance....And there was difference of opinion, and of practice, as to the comparative importance attached to the learning of texts.[1]

It might be remarked here that the Brāhmanical system had given rise to several reactions against its central themes, i.e., *Yajña*, *Mantras* (hymns), *Brahman-Ātman*, *Brāhman*, *Veda-Jñāna* etc., but there was hardly any controversy regarding the significance of renunciation (*Saṁnyāsa*). But the way in which it was understood and absorbed is of considerable significance in assessing its differences from the Vedāntic tradition.

One of the most striking features of Jainism is its uncompromisingly rigorous self-discipline which distinguishes itself from the Brāhmanic tradition. The *Uttarādhyayana-Sūtra* recommends even the mortification of the sage by following the religious practices like *Avamodarika* (taking the least articles of food), *Bhikṣācarya* (severe modes of begging), *Rasatyāga* (abstention from nourishing food), *Kāyakleśa* (self-torturing practices) and *Pratisaṃtinata* (restraints of senses, passions and activities).[2] Professor N. Tatia remarks: "The Jainas, like other exponents of asceticism, endorse suicide in case the body fails to fulfil the demands of the spirit, of course, 'suicide' is a misnomer for this kind of death. It is only an abandonment of the body, unable to help the spirit in its progress....If life helps progress of the spirit, it is to be preserved. If by courting death spiritual fall can be checked, it is welcome."[3] The *Bhagavatī-Sūtra*

---

1. T.W. Rhys Davids, *Buddhist India* (New York : G.P. Putnam's Sons, 1903), p. 159.
2. *Uttarādhyayana-Sūtra*, XXXVI, 249-54; XXI, 4-6.
3. Nathmal Tatia, *Studies in Jain Philosophy* (Banares : Jain Cultural Research Society, 1951), pp. 20-21.

speaks of the two types of renunciation (*Vyutsarga*), namely, *dravyavyutsarga* (renunciation of physical objects like society, articles of food and drink) and *bhāvavyutsarga* (renunciation of four passions, four forms of life and eight *Karma-prakṛtis*).[1] A Jain *yati*, named Skandaka is said to have undergone the vow of continuous fast. His body was reduced to a skeleton but he gained spiritual power (*tapateja*). At last he resolved to give up his body by the *Saṃlekhanā tapa* with the permission of his teacher, Mahāvīra and he courted death.[2]

This ideal of rigorous asceticism is peculiarly Jaina, and even early Buddhism which repudiated the individual soul as a permanent reality did not succumb to this temptation of self-mortification, although it was qualified to do so. The ideal of renunciation bears a somewhat different significance for Buddhism. In the *Kassapa-Sīhanāda-Sutta*, the Buddha does not approve of self-mortification or penance. He rates the inner-discipline, self-victory, charity and freedom from superstitions and automatisms very highly.[3] In the *Udumbarikā-Sīhanāda Suttanta*, the Buddha condemns those *paribbājakas* who have fallen in love with mere asceticism.[4] Here is the apparent distinction between Buddhism and Jainism. Buddhism very clearly denounces the ascetic extravagances of Jainism. There is nevertheless, one characteristic common between both these systems: both of them recommend unconditional and categorical renunciation. Buddhism supports it because it finds life full of suffering without any abiding principle underlying it. Jainism, on the other hand, believes that the *Jiva* (soul) loses its infinite peace, faith, intelligence and power because of its union with matter and *karma* which constitutes *saṁsāra*. Man's personality, for Jainism, consists in its dual nature, i.e., spiritual and material. The course, therefore, open for an ascetic is, to subdue completely the latter so as to help the *Jiva* to return to its inherent glory. This leads to a complete shaking off from *saṁsāra* and *karma*. The rationale

1. Abhayadeva, ed., *Bhagavatī-Sūtra* (Bombay : Agamodaya Samiti, 1921), p. 128b.
2. *Ibid.*, 2.1.94-95.
3. T. W. Rhys Davids, trans. *Dīgha-nikāya* (Oxford : The Clarendon Press, 1899), I, 234 ff.
4. *Ibid.*, III, 43ff, III, 39ff.

of renunciation in both these traditions lies in their life-negating attitude which is further confirmed by their acceptance of the individualistic approach to the religious experience. The final condition for both of them alike is one of inactivity, although it is a life of peace and knowledge. But at any rate, it defeats its own ideal; it results in an *arhata-darśana* or *arhata* ideal. The state of supreme isolation which is the characteristic of Jainism and early Buddhism is represented by the *Tīrthaṁkara* and *Arhata* alike. This spiritual attitude of "isolated, exclusive, alone" lacks in social dimension which is fully brought out in the Vedāntic renunciation.

The fundamental difference between the Vedāntic renunciation and Jain renunciation lies in the fact that in the *Vedānta* it is essential to fulfil the religious duties (*dharma*) which are clearly prescribed by the Vedāntic tradition. These duties are taken to be helpful for cleansing the mind. *Karmas* have been assigned a significant purpose, provided they are performed with proper discipline and training. The *saṁsāra* and *dharma* alike do not create any serious obstacle as they have been brought under the supervision of a transcendental power—the highest Being, as "God" who serves as a ladder for the spiritual progression. In the Vedāntic tradition, renunciation is not merely formal and negative. Renunciation is an enlightened attitude which neither increases nor decreases with the association with either the *saṃsāra* or *karma*. Pointing out the significance of this Vedāntic perspective, H. Zimmer remarks:

> The horizon of sensual experience (*sthūla*) and the domain of inner spiritual event (*sūkṣma*) have both been surpassed. The perfected saint feels himself possessed of an illimited, far-reaching, all-pervading insight...not...of the Jainas and Ājīvakas, but an infallible intuition about things as they occur in everyday situations, or as they are brought to the attention of the saint, the enlightened teacher, in the questions and problems posed to him by the children of the world. This wonderful purity is the most obvious worldly manifestation in him of the fact that he is in perfect harmony with his own Self, unshaken by the gales of passions, uninhibited by the usual limiting qualifications.."[1]

1. Heinrich Zimmer, *Philosophies of India*, ed., Joseph Campbell (Princeton: Princeton University Press, 1969), pp. 452-53.

It will suffice to remark here that the Vedānta does not take *Jīva* (Self)as infinite in number, unlike Jainism. By accepting one ultimate Reality, i.e., *Brahman*, the *Vedānta* does not isolate each of the individual from the generality and universality of the spiritual experience but makes it a part and parcel of it. The realization of this unity is the task of renunciation. Renunciation, therefore, in the *Vedānta*, achieves enormously more than that of the renunciation in Jainism. Renunciation, in the latter, achieves the purity of the *Jiva* whereas in the *Vedānta*, it realizes the whole, beyond which nothing remains. This is a tremendous positive ideal which could be as much this-worldly as other-worldly. Renunciation in Jainism which exhibits an other-worldly nature has finally been overcome. This shows the constant awareness of the positive ideal that the *Vedānta* has in mind.

Renunciation in Ājīvakas

Next to Jainism, *Ājivikism* poses a major threat for the Vedāntic ideal of renunciation. The founder of this religious sect was Maskarin (Mankhali in the *Jain-Prākṛt* and Makkhali in *Pāli*) Gosāla. The word '*Maskarin*' means one who carries a bamboo-staff (*maskara*).[1] A *Maskarin* is also explained as *Ekadaṇḍin*. According to Patañjali, it indicates wandering ascetics who denied the freedom of will.[2] Maskarin Gosāla is considered to be the founder of the religious sect, known as *Ājivika*, although according to the *Bhagavati sūtra*, he was the twenty-fourth *tirthaṁkara* and not the founder of the school. Unfortunately we do not know anything about his predecessors. It is also very difficult to decide the meaning of the term '*Ājivaka*' which has been interpreted differently by various scholars. A.F.R. Hornley explains the word *Ājiva* as "mode of life, or profession, or people".[3] This is also the meaning given to this term in the Sanskrit-English Dictionary of Monnier Williams. As we pointed out earlier, the *Ājivika* school existed at the time

1. *Pāṇini's Grammar*, VI.1.154.
2. A.F.R. Hornley, "Ājīvikas", in James Hastings, ed., *Encyclopaedia of Religion and Ethics* (Edinburgh : T. and T. Clark, 1908), I, 289.
3. *Ibid.*, p. 259.

of the Buddha and Mahāvira and according to G. Buhler, its existence is quite certain by third century B.C.[1]

What concerns us most here is the anti-moralistic and fatalistic doctrine of the *Ājivakas* with which the renunciation doctrine came to be linked in the tradition. Since we do not possess any writings of the *Ājīvakas* we have to content ourselves with some of the citations in books by its opponents. The Buddha criticized the system of Gosāla for preaching 'living in incontinency' (*abrahmacaryavāsa*).[2] The Jain text *Uvāsagadasāo* condemns this school for holding that "there is no such thing as exertion or labour or power or energy or human strength; all things are unalterably fixed."[3] The *Vāyupurāṇa* speaks of the *Ājivaka* as undesirable and unrighteous people who caused a great confusion of *varṇa* and *āśrama.*[4] It also describes it as propounding a theory which lacks in character and moral living.[5] The *Ājīvaka's* theory of self-torturing asceticism and the practice of severe penances as ways to release have also been mentioned in a Tamil text, called, *civaññāna-cittiyana.*[6] The *Ājivakas* are known for their asceticism for acquiring the magical powers. A. L. Basham suggests that Gosāla himself was a magician.[7] They have been described as naked, begging their food and sometimes deliberately starving to death.[8] The Buddhists doubt their asceticism and think that the *Ājivakas* were sensualists and filled with worldliness.[9] Jainism puts forward several objections to them for incurring the sins of immorality, sexuality and drunkenness in order to get artificial pleasure.[10]

The cardinal doctrine of this school is its belief in *niyati* (fatalism). It leaves no scope for spiritual endeavour. A. L. Basham thinks that even Jainism and Buddhism shared its belief

---

1. G. Buhler, "The Barabar and Nagarjuni Hill Cave Inscriptions of Asoka and Dasaratha," *The Indian Antiquary*, XX, pp. 361ff.
2. *Majjhima Nikāya*, 1.541.
3. *Uvāsagadasāo*, 1.97.115.
4. *Adharmikā janāste vai ājīvā vihitāh suraih, Varnāsrāh sankarikāh kāru-silpi janāh. Vāyupurāṇa*, 69.285.
5. *Ibid.*, 69.288-89.
6. M. Mudaliyar, ed., *Civaññāna-Cittiyār* (Madras, 1936), I, 255.
7. A. L. Basham, *History and Doctrines of the Ājivakas* (London: Luzac, 1951), p. 60.
8. *Ibid.*, p. 127 ff.
9. *Ibid.*, p. 123.
10. Jacobi, *Jain Sūtras*, p. 245.

in fatalism[1] but it is very difficult to find evidences to this fact. The logical conclusion of the fatalistic belief has been summed up by H. Zimmer:

> For the *Ājīvaka* doctrine that no amount of moral or ascetic exertion would shorten the series of rebirths offered no hope for a speedy release from the fields of ignorance through saintly exercises. On the contrary, a vast and comprehensive review of all the kingdoms and departments of nature let it appear that each life-monad was to pass, in a series of precisely eightyfour thousand births, through the whole gamut of the varieties of being, starting among the elemental atoms of ether, air, fire, water and earth...each birth being linked to the others in conformity to a precise and minutely graduated order of evolution. All the life-monads in the universe were passing laboriously along this one inevitable way.[2]

Now it is easy to see the religious predicament of the high religious tradition in the face of the heretical movements. It is a fact that the *Ājīvaka* sect was opposed strongly by the Buddha and Mahāvīra alike.[3] The main reason for the opposition was their staunch belief in the law of *Karma* and the necessity of *Mokṣa* or *Nirvāṇa* which was reduced to a status of sheer possibility in the *Ājīvakas*. It is a distinctive mark of the main stream of Indian thought that anything antagonistic to the philosophy of hopefulness was rejected in the long run. A philosophy or religion that fails to inspire a moral and spiritual quest could not flourish for a long time. Renunciation or asceticism, if divorced from the characteristic mode of life and unable to contribute to the unveiling of the glory of life was regarded as sheer waste of time, a merely outward and formal activity.

But here a very important question arises : Was Jainism able to provide a satisfactory substitute for life ? This is a very puzzling question which we have already partly answered. One of the texts of Jainism says : "*Jiva* and non-*jiva* together constitute the universe. If they are separate nothing more is required. If they are united, as they are found in the world, the stoppage

1. *Ibid.*, p. 27 ff.
2. Zimmer, *Philosophies of India*, p. 265.
3. T. W. Rhys Davids, trans; *Aṅguttara Nikāya* (London, 1932), p. 265. The Buddha condemns it for being completely disastrous. And probably the death of Gosāla was caused by Mahavīra's curse.

and the gradual and then final destruction of the union are the only possible ways of considering them."[1] If this is really Freedom, we are tempted to counter that this freedom might be anything but freedom as understood by the *Vedānta*. If renunciation is directed to annihilation of the universe, it is bereft of all implications which are central to it. The sacredness of the universe which originates in the Veda on account of the sacred marriage of Father Heaven and Mother Earth[2] marks a very characteristic development of an early Vedic religion. The blending of the individual world and the cosmic world, resulting in a unique type of synthesis, besides showing that Reality is one, is a Vedāntic doctrine of very positive significance. The *Chāndogya Upaniṣad*[3] indicates it when it asserts that the world has emerged from the One and that that One is one's own self; yet it is not his private or closed self that can explain the Universe but his self as one with the Universal Self. When we consider the nature of renunciation as linked with *Jñāna* for the understanding of the Universal Self which the Vedānta is consistently pointing out, renunciation acquires an entirely different meaning. The Universe is not a bloodless shell which holds life but itself a living reality, completely pervaded by *Ātman* as revealing the entire universe.[4] This perspective is outside the purview of either the Jainas or the *Ājivakas*. Now the only hope would seem to be the theistic schools. Let us see how they assess renunciation in their spiritual schemes of life and if they are any better than the schools we have examined.

Renunciation Among the Theistic Sects

Regarding the theistic implications of renunciation we will turn to some of the sects which are taken to be prevalent at the

---

1. *Tattvārthādhigama-Sūtra*, II, 7.
2. Cf. *Ṛgveda*, 1.89.10.
3. *Ch. Up.*, V. 24.1-2 : *sa ya idam avidvān agnihotram juhoti, yathāṅgārān apohya bhasmani juhuyāt tādṛk tat syāt. atha ya etad evaṁ vidvān agnihotram juhoti, tasya sarveṣu lokeṣu sarveṣu bhuteṣu ātmasu hutam bhavati*. Radhakrishnan, *The Principal Upanisads*, p. 444.
4. Br. Up., II.412 : *sa yathā saindhava-khilya udaka prāsta udakam evānu-vilīyeta na hāsya udgrahaṇāyeva syāt, yato yatas tv ādadīta lavaṇam eva, evam vā are idam mahad bhūtam anantam apāraṁ vijñānaghana eva, etebhyo bhūtebhyaḥ samutthāya, tāny evānuvinaśyati, na pretya samjñāsti, eti are bhavāmi, iti hovāca yājñavalkyaḥ. Ibid.*, p. 200.

time of Śaṁkara. From the literature of the time we come to know that their religious doctrines and practices were criticized from the standpoint of *Vedānta.* The reason for these criticisms in the light of Vedāntic understanding of theistic religions will be examined later. Śaṁkara mentions the *Māheśvaras* who are most probably the same as *Pāśupatas.*[1] Vācaspati Miśra grouped these Māheśvaras into the four, namely, *Śaivas, Pāśupatas, Kāpālikas* and *Kāruṇika-Siddhāntins.*[2] R.G. Bhandarkar thinks that the *Kāṭhaka-Siddhāntins* are none other than the *Kāruṇika-Siddhāntins.*[3] Rāmānuja does not make any difference between these sects which represent the doctrine of Paśupati. In his opinion, these sects are against the Vedic tradition because they make a distinction between the instrumental and material cause (*nimittopādānayorbhedam*) and regard Paśupati as the instrumental cause.[4] It should be noted here that the *Maitrī Upaniṣad* also points to the existence of these sects which distracted the believers in the Veda by their false arguments.[5] The *Mahābhārata* also mentions the Pāśupatas as one of the five schools of religious doctrines.[6] R. G. Bhandarkar places its origin about second century B.C.[7]

Some of the traditional biographies of Śaṁkara give us information about Śaṁkara's encounter with the Buddhists, Jains, *Pāśupatas* and *Kāpālikas* as being some of his rivals. The most important and perhaps the earliest of these biographies are *Śaṁkaravijaya,* atrributed to Ānandagiri and the *Śaṁkaradigvijaya* ascribed to Mādhvācārya (also known as Vidyāraṇya).[8] The legends mentioned in these biographies are mainly three :

---

1. Thibaut, *Vedānta-Sūtras,* II, 435.
2. Bala Sāstrī, ed., *Bhāmati* (Calcutta; Bibliotheca Indica, No. 83, 1880), II.2.37.
3. R. G. Bhandarkar, *Vaisnavism, Saivism and Minor Religious Systems* (Strasbourg : K. J. Trubner 1913), p. 121.
4. P. B. Annangarācārya, ed., *Śrībhāṣya on Brahmasūtra* (Conjeevaram, 1956). II.2.35-37.
5. *Mai. Up.,* VII.8. See Radhakrishnan, *The Principal Upaniṣads,* p. 855.
6. *Śāntiparva,* Ch. 348. v. 64.
7. Bhandarkar, *Vaisnavism, Śaivism etc.,* p. 117.
8. The *Śaṁkara-vijaya* has been edited by Tarkapanchanan and the *Śaṁkara-digvijaya* with Dhanapatisūri's Ḍiṇḍima commentary is *Ānandāsrama* edition.

(a) Śaṁkara's encounter with a treacherous *Kāpālika* named Ugra-Bhairava.
(b) Śaṁkara's battle with the militant Krakaca of Karṇāṭaka and
(c) Śaṁkara's debate with the hedonist Unmatta-Bhairava.

It is difficult to say whether the Vaiṣṇava ascetics also existed at that time and whether Śaṁkara had any encounter with them, although prevalence of *Vaiṣṇavism* in the south cannot be doubted. The cult must have spread but there is no evidence to show at what time it was introduced there. The *Āḷvārs*, the *Saura* sects and the *Tamil Śaivite* saints have also been mentioned at the time of Śaṁkara in his biographies. The sects, we are informed by Bhandarkar had very hostile relations with the Buddhists and Jainas.

Instead of going into the details of their doctrines, let us examine the reasons why Śaṁkara opposed these theistic sects, despite the fact that they were not opposed to Brāhmanism as such and were also ascetic in their life-orientation. Regarding their Brāhmanical nature, S. N. Dasgupta points out :

> The *Pāśupata* system as represented in this work is a Brāhmanical system. For it is only Brahmins who could be initiated to the Pāśupata doctrines but at the same time it seems to break off from Brāhmanism in a variety of ways. It does not recommend any of the Brāhmanical rites but it initiates some new rites and new ways of life which are not so common in the Brāhmanical circle. It keeps some slender contact with Brāhmanism by introducing the meditation on the syllable Om. But as regards many other rituals it seems to be entirely non-vedic.[1]

Their extremely ascetic nature is expressed in the words of Mādhava's *Śaṁkara-digvijaya* :

> After they had been thus repudiated, the various groups (*varṇas*)—*Kāpālikas*, *Cārvākas*, *Saugatas*, *Kṣapaṇakas*, *Jainas* and *Bauddhas*—reappeared in another town....His body was covered with ashes from a funeral pyre; his neck was ringed with a garland of human skulls; (three horizontal) streaks of lamp-black were drawn across his forehead; all his hair was

1. S. N. Dasgupta, *History of Indian Philosophy* (Cambridge : Cambridge University Press, 1955), V, 142-43.

fashioned into a top-knot (*Jaṭā-jūṭa*); his waistband and loincloth were made from a tiger skin; a skull-bowl adorned his left hand; his right hand held a loudly ringing bell (*ghaṇṭā*) and he was chanting repeatedly. O Śambhu Bhairava! Aho, Kālīśa![1]

The classic description of these ascetics is followed by a hedonistic tendency of a *Cārvāka* type. In the *Mālatimādhava* of Bhavabhūti, the Kāpālikas evoke terror (*bhaya*), horror (*bībhatsa*) and disgust (*jugupsā*). Villainous Kāpālika ascetics have been discussed by several Sanskrit dramatists and none of them had any sympathy with them.[2] They have also been shown as having magical powers and command over villainous women with supernatural powers etc.

In the matter of propitiation, they differed from most of the theistic religions. They believed in animal and human sacrifices. "If he (Śiva) does not receive worship with liquor and blood-smeared lotus which are human heads", mentions Mādhava, "how can he attain joy when his body is embraced by the lotus-eyed Umā".[3]

The theological and ritualistic dominance in these sects reduced the nature of philosophy to a secondary status. The doctrine of renunciation (*Saṁnyāsa*) has been taken in its very external form which appears to be superficial. 'For he who is despised, lies happy, freed of all attachment.'[4] And again:

> He should appear as though mad, like a pauper, his body covered with filth letting his beard, nails and hair grow long, without any bodily care. Hereby he becomes cut off from the respectable castes and conditions of men, and the power of passionless detachment is produced.[5]

Associated with the above concept is equally a picture of God as terrifying as it has been presented. Therefore the severe attack of Śaṁkara on these sects should not surprise us.

---

1. XV.28.
2. Keith, *The Sanskrit Drama*, p. 254.
3. Mādhavācarya, *Saṁkarvijaya*, XI.11. See Basham, *History and Doctrines of the Ājīvakas*, p. 114.
4. B.H.H. Ingalls, "Cynics and Pāśupatas: The Seeking of Dishonour", *Harvard Theological Review*, LV, p. 286.
5. *Ibid.*

Renunciation in Buddhism

We propose now to discuss the Buddhist attitude towards renunciation because Buddhism in its original form belongs with other Indian traditions in respect of ideas pertaining to renunciation which is aimed at freedom from the cycle of *Karma-Saṁsāra*. What interests us most here is the examination of such a religious system like Buddhism, advocating renunciation despite the fact that it has no place either for the individual soul or the universal soul. Here there is nothing like essential, permanent Reality : everything is subject to the continuous flux—"no kernel which remains when the husk has been removed; there is nothing but husk. Nor is there any kernel hidden away behind the phenomenon of the world."[1] The rationale of renunciation, therefore, in Buddhism does not derive from the quest for or realization of *Brahman* or *Īśvara* but elimination of suffering (*dukkha*), recognized as the greatest evil, having its source in the desire for existence. Pointing out the place of *dukkha* in Buddhism, Gunaratne remarks:

> The word 'dukkha' must awaken in our minds not only thoughts of pain and distress, but also all these thoughts about the unsatisfactory and illusory nature of the things of this world, their unsubstantiality, their failure to satisfy completely, and their inevitable ending in disappointment, sorrow and disharmony. Dukkha consists of that state of unbalance that continued agitation and disturbance... Perhaps the word 'disharmony' can be regarded as the closest equivalent of *dukkha*.[2]

On the question of *dukkha*, there is hardly any disagreement in the Indian philosophical system. Also there is unanimity on the question of release from *dukkha*. All the systems agree that there is a state which is possible to attain and that state is free from suffering. Renunciation is indispensible for reaching the state of freedom, whether it is called *Mokṣa, Kaivalya* or *Nirvāṇa*. By associating the concept of impermanence (aniccā, *anitya*) with renunciation, Buddhism reversed the traditional teaching of *Brahmanism* which directed the principle

1. Farquhar, *The Religious Quest of India*, p. 105.
2. V. F. Gunaratne, *The Significance of the Four Noble Truths* (Kandy : B.P.S., 1968), p. 8.

of *saṁnyāsa* towards uncovering of the permanent (*nitya*) Self (*ātman*). If all things in the world are transient and unsubstantial, our spiritual endeavours are sheer waste. But to say so would be a kind of injustice to the spirit of Buddhism. For it admits that nothing that we do disappears without leaving its consequences behind, but can such a doctrine be reconciled with the denial of an enduring self? Paul Deussen hints at the same problem when he says: 'This *karman* must have in every case an individual bearer and that is what the *upaniṣads* call *ātman* and what the Buddhists inconsistently deny.'[1] Without denying the spiritual contribution of Buddhism, it seems clear to us that the metaphysical considerations centering around the denial of Ultimate Reality, label Buddhism as very pessimistic and negative. The doctrine of unsubstantiality and temporality when pushed further by Nāgārjuna established pure and simple illusoriness of all phenomena.[2] Since a general principle of Reality in Buddhism was apparently suspended, renunciation could not serve a very positive function. One thing stands clear that for the *Vedānta*, the direction was provided by *Śruti* (Revelation) but Buddhism in the absence of it found it difficult to provide a direction to philosophy at least for some time.

The philosophy of *Bhūta-tathatā* of Aśvaghoṣa marks a clear departure from pure phenomenalism to monistic idealism. Aśvaghoṣa admitted one permanent reality from which he sought to derive everything else. S. N. Dasgupta remarks: "Aśvaghoṣa seems to combine these two ideas into the doctrine that there is a reality which he calls the mere thatness, of which it is not possible to make any kind of affirmation or negation; and following the footsteps of the *Upaniṣads*, he describes it as forming the essential nature of the soul."[3] The term '*tathatā*' (suchness) here means "oneness of all things" which can be realized by *Jñāna* and *saṁnyāsa* which remove the functioning of *avidyā*. *Avidyā* serves as a positive entity in the sense of false

1. Paul Deussen, *Indian Antiquary*, (1900), p. 398.
2. Śaṁkara, on this account does not find any need for serious refutation of this doctrine. It stands self-refuted. See Thibaut, *The Vedānta Sūtras*, II, 427. Even Jainism finds Nāgārjuna's philosophy nihilistic.
3. S. N. Dasgupta, *Indian Idealism* (Cambridge: The University Press, 1933), p. 90.

knowledge in the same way as the world serves as a positive entity in the sense of false knowledge. *Jñāna* and even *saṁnyāsa* cannot work in a vacuum. The contribution of Aśvaghoṣa lies in providing a structure to Buddhism which enriched the social dimension; the dimension which was otherwise lacking in the early Buddhism.[1] This phase of thought had its further repercussions. Buddhism seems to have adopted almost the same pattern of Renunciation, namely cosmic and acosmic with its implications for faith, devotion etc. Śāntideva, for example, incorporates 'faith' into Buddhism.[2]

We have so far spoken about the main traditions of renunciation, which, though they manifest some common characteristics, are yet different in fundamental respects. We have endeavoured, throughout, to show, directly or indirectly, that in spite of certain ascetic extravagances (which can be legitimately expected in such a vast tradition), there is a dominant tendency towards a positive reconstruction of the doctrine of renunciation, which has been, strangely enough, shared by all. I do not mean to imply that it has never acquired a negative or life-denying tendency but I want to assert here that this tendency has always been resisted and could not be allowed to flourish without dissensions within the given tradition or outside it. We have noticed the sharp reaction by Buddhism and Jainism alike against the *Ājīvakism*. We have also noticed the criticisms levelled against each other by the Buddhists and Jainas. We have examined, though very briefly, the transformation within the Buḍdhist tradition itself—the transformation which is essential for keeping the religion alive. This phenomenon is equally true for Brāhmanism. In my opinion no tradition has undergone such a degree of modifications as Brāhmanism has. And perhaps no tradition has aroused such a vast controversy, appreciation and condemnation as Brāhmanism has. It was criticized not only by those systems

1. B. G. Tilak thinks that this transformation in the Mahāyāna Buddhism could only be possible because of the impact of the *Gītā*. He cites several internal and external evidences to prove this thesis. See *Gītā Rahasya*, pp. 801-815.

2. *Śraddhā-mūlam dṛḍhīkṛtya bodhau kāryā matirdṛḍhā. Śāntideva's Śikṣāsamuccaya.* See, Cecil Bendall and Rouse, eds., *Śāntideva's Śikṣāsamuccaya* (London, 1922), p. 2.

which were outside that tradition but also by the tradition itself. Yet it is understandable that the rationale of renunciation differed from system to system but it is curious enough that no system could ever emancipate itself from the phenomenon of renunciation. It is not as simple as it appears to be. The goal that is reached in the Indian tradition, in general, is through renunciation which is characterized, on the one hand, by *Jñāna* and the metaphysical structure, on the other. The spiritual history of India indicates that whenever the power of the ideal of renunciation weakened and the pursuit of *Jñāna* and Ultimate Reality were undertaken in disregard of it, there has occurred a noticeable decline in philosophic thought as well as deterioration in the fabric of religion. And contrariwise, whenever the spirit of renunciation revived itself, the foundations were always *Jñāna* and the discovery of its metaphysical ground. I have, obviously in mind, the spread of the Mahāyāna Buddhism and the *Vedānta*. It is impossible for historians, to speak with certainty as to which of these the positive ideal of renunciation belongs. It seems it belongs to both of them equally. In this respect as well as in other respects there seems to be a constant overlapping of these two traditions.

Chapter Three

METAPHYSICAL FOUNDATION OF RENUNCIATION

Problem of Self-knowledge

In the previous chapter we briefly referred to the fact that renunciation in the *Vedānta* has its root in the metaphysical structure of Reality and *Jñāna*. Although these two elements are common to all Indian thought nowhere have they been so forcefully brought out as in the *Vedānta*. The *Vedānta* may accordingly be taken to represent the consummation of Indian thought. On the theoretical side, it is based on the Upaniṣadic doctrine of *Brahman*, which is to be approached only through *jñāna* or *gnosis*, and on the practical side, the pursuit of *mokṣa* as the final culmination of *saṁnyāsa*. These two characteristics also signify the fact that the *Vedānta* is neither a pure intellectualism nor a simple moralism. To understand either *Brahman* or *Saṁnyāsa* in the ordinary logical and ethical sense will be a grave injustice to the spirit of the *Vedānta*.[1] But it should be equally remembered here that these are the means of attaining the final ideal. In other words, the value and validity of experience, action and morality can be legitimately accepted within *Vedānta* so far as they seek to interpret and help the spiritual goal of life but

1. "The logical faculty of thought (if I may be allowed such an expression)", says S. N. Dasgupta, "always seeks to break up the immediacy of anything that is given, into differences, and then guided by any particular kind of interest to pick up any of these and unite them with other entities, similarly broken up and abstracted from other unities. When our experiences remain as mere immediacies, or felt wholes of the moment, they remain shut within ourselves; conceived as such, these are isolated facts which can seldom be connected up with one another. Each felt whole stands alone by itself." S. N. Dasgupta, *Philosophical Essays* (Calcutta: University of Calcutta, 1941), p. 71. Morality, in the same way, it might be added, however much it may widen our outlook, keeps us divided from the rest of mankind. The essential duality of the moral world can only be transcended by a man who is truly free. This can only be possible when he rises above the anthropocentric view and establishes his identity with the Reality, based on the Vedāntic ideal of human unity.

they cannot be regarded as substitutes for it. What is sufficient is the self-knowledge backed by revelation (*śruti*). J.G. Arapura's following statement is closely related to the subject under consideration :

> Transcendent self-knowledge and revelation constitute the two Archimedean points in religion's own epistemology. Undoubtedly, even Buddhism as religion—which it is—is based on these two, a matter that can be convincingly demonstrated by a correct study of the sources of authoritative knowledge in the Buddhist texts . . .that the Upaniṣads present the most perfectly consistent and by far the most thoroughly developed doctrines of the Self and Self-knowledge is indisputable. (Buddhism must be understood as representing the diverse side of these doctrines, and in the last resort as making them more meaningful by challenging them to their ultimate foundations and hence radicalizing them). And a goodly position of these famous sacred texts are about these. Because of its wholly transcendent character, knowledge of the self can be appropriated, it is argued by Yājñavalkya, the greatest of its spokesmen, only negatively as *neti neti* (not this, not this). The highest expression of this line of thought is found in the greatest Upaniṣadic text of all which says *tat tvam asi* (That art Thou). But such a knowledge, it is also said elsewhere, does not come except through revelation, as stated in the *Kaṭha Upaniṣad* (I. 2.23): "This self cannot be attained by instruction nor by intellectual power, nor even through much hearing. It is to be attained only by the one whom he (the Self) chooses. To such a one the Self reveals its own nature."[1]

The present chapter confines itself to the understanding of this Self-knowledge and its implications for renunciation. If the knowledge (*Jñāna*) of *Brahman* in the *Vedānta* necessarily culminates in renunciation, it should not imply, as has been throughout pointed out, the denial of all given reality as this denial is anything but vedāntic. The denial of 'givenness', *a priori*, rests upon a reality behind the self-descrepant givenness. Viewed in this light, *Brahman* only appears as the world. It is the original

1. Arapura, *Religion as Anxiety and Tranquillity*, p. 38.

of which the world (the givenness), as S. Radhakrishnan puts it, may be regarded as "translation at the plane of space-time."[1] It is in the sense that Śaṁkara's philosophy can be differentiated from the *Śūnyavāda* of Nāgārjuna. Here the remark of Hiriyanna may be noted:[2]

> If according to the *Mādhyamika* it is impossible for thought to rest in the relative, it is equally impossible for it according to Śaṁkara, to rest in absolute nothing. To use the terminology of the Upaniṣads, the *Advaita* denies "names" and "forms", but not that which appears under their guise, or as an old writer has observed while the *Advaitin* negates only distinction (*bheda*), the *Mādhyamika* negates it as well as the distincts (*bhidyamāna*).

The Advaitic acceptance of Reality behind the empirical phenomena—the Reality which is utterly ungiven, i.e., as self-luminous (*svayamprabhā*) is an immediate certainty, denial of which is sheer impossibility as the denial in itself postulates it.[3] Knowledge, according to the *Vedānta* is foundational and is the necessary condition of all existence. Vidyāraṇya, the author of the *Pañcadaśī* also postulates such a knowledge (*saṁvid*) as a necessary pre-condition of all existence.[4] As a necessary pre-condition of all existence, this knowledge (*Jñāna*) is called *advitīyaṁ* (without a second) and *amṛtaṁ* (immortal). Because of its non-duality, it forms an absolute unity.

> For where there is duality as it were, there one smells another, there one hears another, there one speaks to another,

---

1. Radhakrishnan, *Indian Philosophy*, II, 570.
2. Hiriyanna, *Indian Philosophy*, p. 373. Also,

   Nāsato vidyate bhāvo nābhāvo vidyate sataḥ /
   ubhayorapi dṛṣṭo'ntas tvanayostattvadarśibhiḥ//
   Bhagavad-Gītā, II. 16.

   Bhagavad-Gītā Śāṁkarabhāṣya: *tadāsatve sarvābhāvaprasaṅga iti cet na. Yadāviṣaya buddhir na vyabhicarati tat sat, yadāviṣya vybhicarati tat asat*. See Mahadeva Sastry, *The Bhagavad-Gītā*, pp. 34-37.
3. *Sarvo hi ātmāstitvam pratyeti na nāhamasmīti. Yadi hi nātmāstitvaprasiddhiḥ syāt sarvo loko nāhamasmīti pratīyāt*. George Thibaut, *Vedānta Sūtras*, I, 9-15.
4. See Hariprasad Shastri, trans; *Pañcadaśī* : *A Treatise on Advaita Metaphysics of Swāmī Vidyāraṇya* (London: Shanti Sadan, 1956), p. 9. For a good introduction see Abhedananda, *An Introduction to the Philosophy of Pañcadaśī* (Calcutta, 1948).

there one thinks of another, there one understands another. Where verily, everything has become the Self when by what and whom should one smell, then by what and whom should one see, then by what and whom should one hear, then by what and to whom should one speak, then by what and on whom should one think, then by what and whom should one understand? By what should one know that by which all this is known? By what my dear, should one know the knower?[1]

The above passage metaphysically indicates that there can be no object of knowledge without *Jñāna* and *Jñāna* which is a pre-condition of everything cannot be an object of knowledge—a contention that establishes the view that *Jñāna* (*Caitanya*) is the prius of reality. Śaṁkara in his commentary on *Kenopaniṣad* calls it *nirupādhika* (unconditional) and the essence of *Ātman*.[2] He bases his philosophy on the soteriological function of knowledge: "Save for that, nothing is worth knowing".[3] "Knowledge here is transformed into a meditation", remarks M. Eliade, and metaphysics becomes soteriology. In India not even "logic" is without a soteriological function in its beginnings. Manu uses the term *ānvikṣikī* ("science of controversy" logic) as an equivalent to *ātma-vidyā* ("knowledge of the soul" *ātman*)—that is, to metaphysics."[4]

The one legitimate conclusion that follows from the above discussion is that the self-knowledge which is soteriological in the *vedānta*, is transcendent to thought and that it cannot be conceived in terms of the empirical. But it should not mean that empirical knowledge in the *Vedānta* is discarded. As indicated earlier, empirical knowledge would be impossible without there being infinite consciousness at the back of it. Therefore every knowledge presupposes self-knowledge without exhausting it. To put it simply, such knowledge serves to reveal, though partially, the metaphysical knowledge but does not represent it. And

---

1. Radhakrishnan, *The Principal Upaniṣads*, p. 201.

2. M. Hiriyanna, trans., *Śaṁkarācārya's Kenopaniṣadbhāṣya* (Srirangam, 1915) P. 1.

3. *etad jñeyaṁ nityam evātmasaṁsthaṁ nātaḥ paraṁ veditavyaṁ hi kiñcit.*—*Śvet. Up.* 1.12. Radhakrishnan, *The Principal Upanisads*, p. 716.

4. M. Eliade, *Yoga: Immortality and Freedom*, trans. Willard R. Trask (Princeton: Princeton University Press, 1969), p. 13.

exactly is the same case with regard to the empirical things. In other words, the whole complex of knowledge and phenomenal existents is based on the delusive structure of *vṛtti-jñāna* (reason) which because of its inherent procedure understands the unconditioned as conditioned and equates the empirical with the metaphysical.[1] The *Vedānta* rejects this confusion and in doing so, it does not reject or displace anything but only the misconception about it. The rejection of this confusion is done for soteriological reasons because every empirical knowledge, whether of the universe, society, morality or ethics, in the form in which it is experienced by us, is due to the lack of self-knowledge which results in isolating the realm of experience from its basis, i.e., *Brahman* and mistaking the 'isolation' or 'abstraction' for the real. The *Jñāna* that is capable of removing this metaphysical error, is the very nature of the self but appears to have been forgotten for the time being. The task of *saṁnyāsa* lies in installing the forgotten self-knowledge. The task is accomplished not by isolating the world from its source or renouncing it (as is the case with some of the religious systems as discussed earlier). All that is needed is the removal of the self-ignorance (*ātma-ajñāna*) through its contrary (*ātman-jñāna*).

The reasons for taking this position are two-fold: firstly the *vedānta* is not a negative doctrine which is throughout evident in its metaphysical structure. In fact, it is a reaction against any negative philosophy or religion, whether heterodox or orthodox. Wherever the *Vedānta* explains *Brahman* in negative terms, it is done, directly or indirectly along with the positive ones, like *Aham brahma asmi* (I am Brahman), *tat tvam asi* (That thou art). The meanings of these statements again do not lie outside the realm of experience nor are they completely axiologi-

---

1. "There are these two principles, the principle of revelation and all that which is revealed by it; it alone is real and in the highest and truest sense. It is absolute in the sense that there is no growth, decay, evolution or change in it, and it is perfectly complete in itself. It is infinite in the sense that no finite can form part of it, though through it all finitude is being constantly revealed. It is all-pervading in the sense that no spatial or temporal limits can be said to affect it in any way, though all these are being constantly revealed by it. It is neither in my head nor in my body nor in the space before me; but yet there is nowhere that it is not. It has sometimes been designated as the "Self" or *ātman*, but only in the sense of denoting its nature as the supreme essence and transcendent reality of all—the *Brahman*." Dasgupta, *History of Indian Philosophy*, II, 16.

cally other to it, as we will examine in the life of the *Jivan-mukta* (enlightened in life time). The *Brahma-Jñāna* (Self-knowledge) constitutes the whole of experience, either on the subject or object side. It is only with reference to this spiritual experience that the *Vedānta* constitutes the consummation of the integral experience. J.G. Arapura's following remark substantiates it :

> Integral experience is the fulness of mystical intuition, reason and feeling. It is visualized as the completion of all of them, in their togetherness and integrity. As such it is religious experience in the highest and completest sense. It is the fulfilment of mysticism. Now there are three aspects in this fulfilment and completion of mysticism by integral experience. (1) In the place of mystical intuition, we have the whole of a person's powers, including mystical intuition organized around it. (2) In the place of the Absolute Beyond, we have the Absolute conceived as the unity of the Beyond and the universe. (3) In the place of objectivity or otherness, we have the integrity of subject and object. All these are really aspects of the problem of transcendence and immanence.[1]

Secondly, if the metaphysical foundation of the *Vedānta* is based on the positive ideal of the integral experience of *Brahman*, the understanding of the principle of renunciation as a sole means of the realization of such a unity, must be positive. In the absence of this approach, it would rather defeat its own ideal. Needless to say, a resistance against the negative ideal of renunciation is the central motif of the *Dharmaśāstra*, the Mahāyāna Buddhism and the *Vedānta*. In the *Vedānta* directly and in the Mahāyāna Buddhism perhaps indirectly, it was found necessary to understand the Ultimate Reality and renunciation not by isolating them from the universe but by making them the ground or substratum (*pratiṣṭhā*) of the universe.[2] The spiritual

1. J. G. Arapura, *Radhakrishnan and Integral Experience* (New York: Asia Publishing House, 1966), p. 97.

2. *tathāgato yatsvabhāvas tatsvabhāvam idaṁ jagat.* *Mk.* XXII. 16 quoted by Murti, *The Central Philosophy of Buddhism*, p. 233.

Also *vidyāpi sarveṣām satyādipadānām lakṣyam ekam eva nirviśeṣaṁ brahma, tathāpi nivarttanīyāṁśādhikena na padāntaravaiyarthyam.* See T. R. V. Murti, "The Two Definitions of *Brahman* in *Advaita*" *K. C. Bhattacharya Memorial Volume* (Amalner, 1958), p. 150.

technique of renunciation was directed to this central point of making the renunciants the "support" of the universe. Here the philosophical attitude is generated purely by *jñāna* (metaphysical knowledge). Śaṁkara has throughout made this point very clear.[1] Renunciation, therefore is not withdrawal in the ordinary sense. Strictly speaking, it is withdrawal from the imperfect aspect of the world which constitutes the profane existence by means of *Jñāna*, by already participating in a mode of sanctified existence of which we are assured by the *Śruti* (revelation). In the absence of this assurance, the categorical and unconditional renunciation could have been possible which is certainly not the case with the *Vedānta*. The unity ideal which is the express motif of the Vedānta itself is opposed to the negative ideal of renunciation. The ideal of renunciation is central to the realization of a positive nature of inexpressible happiness. In a word, it is participation in *Brahman*. Let us more closely examine the implications of the *māyā* doctrine in the Advaita Vedānta to see whether there can be any illusion without a basis in Reality or substratum (*sadadhiṣṭhāna*).

Māyā, Brahman and Saṁnyāsa

The ontological position of the Advaita Vedānta has been indicated in dealing with the problem of Self-knowledge. The object of right knowledge is *Brahman* who is the integral part of one's nature. Renunciation, therefore, metaphysically speaking, is not the renunciation of one's real nature, as something that is real cannot be renounced or abandoned. What is being renounced or abandoned is ignorance (*avidyā*). The fact that *avidyā* is a power inherent in the *Brahman* shows that it is dependent thereon. In other words, *avidyā* itself belongs to *Brahman*,

1. "Without our participation in the Divine" remarks S. Radhakrishnan, "neither knowledge of God nor love of God is possible... To know this Self and made this knowledge effective in human life has been the aim of man, according to the *Vedānta* System." S. Radhakrishnan, trans., The *Brahma Sūtra*. (London: George Allen and Unwin Ltd., 1960), p. 126.

as only a conscious being capable of knowledge can be ignorant.[1] Understood accordingly, renunciation at the individual level, is only the correction or the error-removing form of the individual and in a sense is even a technique to preserve the glory and purity of the individual. Manu remarks : "If he keeps both his organs and his consciousness under subjection, he can attain his goal without tormenting his body."[2] One of the *Upaniṣads* says : "The knots in the heart are cut asunder, all doubts are completely eliminated, all forms fade away, when one sees the *ātman*."[3]

Renunciation does not mean, therefore, lack of constant vigilance and retirement into the barren life of isolation but perfecting oneself by subduing those impressions and desires of life which are life-negating by strong personal effort. "He who is free from self-sense, whose understanding is not sullied, though he slays these people, he slays not nor is he bound (by his actions)".[4] And further, "But a man of disciplined mind, who moves among the objects of sense, with the senses under control and free from attachment and aversion, he attains purity of spirit."[5]

It is well to remember in this connection that, according to the *Vedānta*, *ajñāna* or nescience exists in the pure self which is its locus. The cessation of *ajñāna* is not the cessation of the self and therefore it will be wrong to say that *ajñāna* is mere misconception or wrong notion (*viparyaya* of Nāgārjuna). Here it is a positive power (*avidyā-śakti*). *Brahman* with its *avidyā* is regarded as the material cause of the world (*avidyā-sahita-brah-*

1. *śaktir ity ātma-para-tantratayā ātmanaḥ sarvakāryopādānasya nirodhṛtvam*. See Prakāśātman, *Pañca-pādikā-vivaraṇa* (Banaras: the Vizianagram Sanskrit Series, 1892), p. 13.

2. Buhler, *The Laws of Manu*, p. 48.

3. *bhidyate hṛdayagranthiś chidyante sarva-saṁśayāḥ kṣīyante cāsya karmāṇi tasmin dṛṣṭe parāvare*. *Muṇ. Up.* II. 2.9.

4. *Yasya 'nāhaṁkṛto bhāvo buddhir yasya na lipyate, hatvā'pi sa imāṁ lokān na hanti na nibadhyate*. *Gītā*, XVIII, 17. S. Radhakirshnan, *The Bhagavadgītā* (London: George Allen & Unwin Ltd., 1948) p. 357.

5. *rāgadveṣaviyuktaistu viṣayān indriyaiścaran, ātmavaśyair vidheyātmā prasādam adhigacchati*. *Gītā*, II. 64. *Ibid*., 126.

mopādānam).[1] *Jñāna*, therefore, aims at the proper discrimination between *Brahman* and *ajñāna*, hence the exhortation that one shall have an initial sense of discrimination of the eternal one and non-eternal (*nityānityavastuviveka*).[2] *Avidyā or ajñāna* is not simple absence of knowledge, a mere state of privation. It is what masquerades as knowledge of the Real, while in itself it is but ignorance. It is an appearance (*mithyā*), neither unreal nor again real. It is associated with the Self in the form of sub-conscious impressions (*vāsanās*) and apotheosised as the congenital feeling of I-ness (*vāsanā-ahaṁkāra-sahitam*). When *Jñāna* removes *ajñāna*, the latter is said to be cancelled as such (*bādha*) by which is implied that it is transformed. The 'falsity' of its claim, its "bluff" is called off and pure knowledge that stands underlying it, illumining it, emerges to the surface. Such an interpretation is quite in keeping with the general trend of the Vedāntic thought according to which the world is not negated at the dawn of knowledge. It is simply re-interpreted as *Brahman*. This position also has its implication for renunciation. Renunciation, being grounded in the *Jñāna*, should not be taken for the rejection of the world but for the re-interpretation of it. If this position is not taken into consideration then the Upaniṣadic assertion that the *Brahman* is the ground of the world loses its significance. If *Brahman* is only real and interprets the world as the cause of it, the world is unreal in the sense of the absence of knowledge and not wrong knowledge. If the world is taken in the latter sense, it cannot be associated with *Brahman*. But the world as absence of knowledge indicates the limitation of *Brahman* due to certain impositions. When these impositions are removed by *Jñāna*, the world is realized as identical with *Brahman*. A right realization of *aham brahma asmi* or *tat tvam asi* dispels only falsity of knowledge and is of

1. Appaya Dikṣita, *Siddhāntaleśa* (The Vizianagaram Sanskrit Series, 1890), p. 12.

2. Śaṁkara's Comm., *Brahma-sūtras*, 1.1.1. It is useful to note here that Śaṁkara uses the term '*nitya*' as a synonym of *sat* or *satya* and *anitya*, as its opposite. The point is that it is the same manner of 'opposition' (*virodha*) that the terms *jñāna* and *ajñāna* too should be understood. For details also see Swami Madhvananda, trans., *The Vivekacudāmaṇi of Sri Śaṁkarācārya* (Calcutta: Advaita Ashram, 1970), Śloka, 19, p. 7.

greater significance than dispelling the world-existence. It is easy to see that this view of *ajñāna* has a positive significance and does not ignore the philosophical understanding of the phenomenal world which is not an object of the *jñāna-abhāva* but *mithyā-jñāna*. The world is not merely a subjective sensation or false idea but it has a status which can be further enriched by removing *avidyā* associated with it in the scheme of the metaphysical knowledge in order to realize its original purity. It must be noted, however, that Śaṁkara's own writings do not always give a clue to this type of understanding and there are many passages which are explicitly against our interpretation but the general tendency of his thought cannot be quite irrelevant to the approach under consideration. "We cannot define *Brahman*" says T.R.V. Murti, "except as the reality of the world, or as what the world is mistaken for. The nature of the mistake and the way to remove it is therefore necessarily a preliminary part for the quest of *Brahman*. . . .It is literally an uncovering or unmasking process. Self-realization is a case of gaining depth without adding to our stock of knowledge (*abheyānupādeya*). Brahman-knowledge is insight, not information."[1]

The doctrine of *Māyā* has been developed to account for the cosmic implications of Advaita Vedānta. In this sense *Māyā* is often referred to a *Prakṛti* (cosmic world), but its significance and unity rest on *Brahman* and in this sense it is different from the *Prakṛti* of the *Sāṁkhya*. The sole object of explaining the cosmic world and this manner is to provide it a significant status for realization of *Brahman*.[2] The remark of J.G. Arapura substantiates the above consideration:

> *Māyā* theory has implications for several things, mainly experience, the world and language. The original motivation in articulating the theory was to rationalise these implications by making them cohere with the fundamental metaphysical position of Advaita Vedānta. . . . But then such a

---

1. Murti, *Bhattacharya Memorial Volume*, p. 137.

2. *Brahmaṇo jagadākāraparīyṇā mi vādi yacchrūyate tadabrahmadarśanopāyatvenaiva viniyaujyate.* *Brahmasūtra Śāṁkarabhāṣya.* Cf. M.S. Bakre, ed. *Brahmasūtrabhāṣya, with Ratnaprabhā, the Bhāmatī and Nyāyanirṇaya* (Bombay: Nirnayasagara Press, 1934), p. 381.

> rational post script has been necessary not only for theoretical considerations but for existential ones as well. It must never be lost sight of that the *Vedānta*, like most other Indian systems, is not only philosophy, but also religion.[1]

The existential and religious implications of the *Māyā* doctrine as suggested by Arapura can be clearly linked with the *Saṁnyāsa* doctrine of the Advaita Vedānta. In order to understand this position more clearly, let us turn to the metaphysical mechanism of *Māyā* in Advaita Vedānta. Pointing out the origin of *Māyā*, R.D. Ranade remarks:

> There are, on the whole, three different theories which try to account for the doctrine of Māyā, as found in Śaṁkara and later writers, in different ways. According to the first, the doctrine of Māyā is mere fabrication of the fertile genius of Śaṁkara: according to the second, the doctrine of Māyā as found in Śaṁkara is to be traced entirely to the influence of the Śūnyavāda of the Buddhists; according to the third Śaṁkara's doctrine of Māyā is to be found already full-fledged in the Upaniṣads, of which he is merely an exponent.[2]

Without going into the details of the controversy, it seems correct to hold that Śaṁkara being the exponent of the *Upaniṣads*, developed this doctrine further. The Ground, i. e., *Brahman* of the Universe as covered by the beginningless *Māyā*, has been discussed by the *Īśa Upaniṣad*.[3] Some of the *Upaniṣads*, like the *Bṛhadāraṇyaka*[4] and the *Śvetāśvatara*[5] point out that significance of God in the cessation of Māyā.

---

1. J. G. Arapura, "Māyā and the Discourse about Brahman" in Sprung, ed., *The Problem of Two Truths in Buddhism and Vedānta*, p. 110.

2. Ranade, *A Constructive Survey of Upanisadic Philosophy*, p. 162.

3. *hiraṇmayena pātreṇa satyasyāpihitaṁ mukham tat tvaṁ pūṣan apāvṛṇu satyadharmāya dṛṣṭaye.* (The face of truth is covered with a golden disc. Unveil it, O Pūsan, so that I who love the truth may see it.) *Īśa Up.* 15. Radhkrishnan, *The Principal Upanisads*, p. 577.

4. *Asato mā sad gamaya, tamaso mā jyotirgamaya, mṛtyormāmṛtaṁgamaya. Bṛ. Up.* 1.3.28.

5. "What is perishable is the *Pradhāna* (primary matter). What is immortal and imperishable is *Hara* (the Lord). Over both the perishable and the soul, the one God rules. By meditating on Him, by uniting with Him, by reflecting on His beingmore and more, there is complete cessation from the illusion of the world ' *Śvet. Up.* I.10. Radhakrishnan, p. 715.

Māyā, therefore is the power of God and it is of a positive nature which assigns a degree of reality to the cosmic world. The Advaitic writers from Śaṁkara onwards have maintained the empirical reality of the world. This has been possible by approaching the problem of the Ultimate Reality fundamentally from two standpoints, i.e., *svarūpalakṣaṇa* (essential standpoint) and *taṭasthalakṣaṇa* (accidental point of view).[1]

The Vedāntic stand on the two definitions of *Brahman* and their roles in the Advaitic metaphysics is of a great significance. For this reason, any attempt to discard the spirit of advaitism on the basis of its condemnation of the world as false without properly understanding it, is sheer injustice to this system of thought. This explains why Śaṁkara attaches so much significance to the *taṭasthalakṣaṇa* according to which *Brahman* is the cause (*kāraṇa*) of the origin, sustenance and destruction of the world.[2] The Vedānta clearly establishes the fact that God alone is the cause of the world and refutes the theories of the *Nyāya-Vaiśeṣika* and the *Sāṁkhya*. What assigns reality to this world is *Īśvara* who is a truth of the greatest spiritual significance. Śaṁkara seeks the support of the *Upaniṣads* in order to explain that the *nirguṇa* (acosmic) and *saguṇa* (cosmic) *Brahman* are not two *Brahmans* but only one as viewed from the two standpoints. T.R.V. Murti elucidates:

> As in the case of the Absolute, the doctrine of two truths also is liable to misinterpretation. There are not two different spheres or sets of objects to which they apply. There would then be no point in calling one *samvṛti* and the other

1. tatra lakṣaṇaṁ dvividhaṁ svarūpalakṣaṇaṁ taṭasthalakṣaṇañca iti. See S. S. Sastri, ed., *Vedāntaparibhāṣā of Dharmarāja* (Madras: The Adyar Library, 1942), p. 114.

Śaṁkara falls back on the authority of the *Upaniṣads* which describe the absolute as acosmic (*niṣprapañca*) and cosmic (*saprapañca*). See *Bṛ. Up.* III, viii, and *Ch. Up.* III. xiv. According to Śaṁkara, these two approaches have also been taken by Bādarāyaṇa in the *Vedānta Sūtras* (III. ii. ii). These views, namely, *svarūpalakṣaṇa* (acosmic) and *taṭasthalakṣaṇa* (cosmic) are about the same Reality, and the apparent distinction between the two is due to the difference in standpoint.

2. *Janmādyasya yataḥ—Vedānta Sūtra*, 1.1.2. See Thibaut, *The Vedānta Sūtra*, I, 15-22.

paramārtha; the two might be different, but one would not be less real than the other. The difference is in the manner of our apprehension: one is the *tattva* which is the object of right knowledge and the other is the object of false knowledge. In fact, there is only one Truth—the *paramārtha-satya*, as there is only one real—the Absolute. The other *saṁvṛti-satya*, is truth so-called in common parlance, it is totally false from the absolute standpoint.[1]

The purpose of the *Māyā* theory is to enable the *sādhaka* to unveil the nature of absolute truth, though unknown and believed not to be knowable but as demanding to be known. The realization of the truth, as we pointed out earlier necessarily implies the grace of *Īśvara* and dedication to him. The acceptance of God in Advaita presupposes renunciation of worldly life (the life of pragmatic utility). "For the *aparā-vidyā*", says Rudolf Otto, "Śaṁkara is a passionate theist. If he was the greatest teacher of his time, the restorer of the pure Vedāntic doctrine, the antagonist and destroyer of sects, false teacher and mistaken philosophers—particularly the Buddhists—he was this in the name of *Brahman* whose foremost and fundamental definition reads thus: *Brahman* is that from which the origin, continuance and dissolution of the world comes. That is, he is a world-creating, world-sustaining and world-dissolving God."[2]

From the above standpoint, it may be said here that Śaṁkara's contribution lies in the fact that while agreeing fully that *Jñāna* alone can bring liberation, he has recognized the significance of actions and duties of the orders of life as helpful for the dawn of knowledge. Here the ultimate model is *Īśvara*.[3]

1. T.R.V Murti, "Samvṛti and Paramārtha", in Sprung, ed., *The Problem of Two Truths in Buddhism and Vedānta*, p. 19.

2. Rudolf Otto, *Mysticism East and West*, trans. E.L. Bracey and R.C. Payne (New York: Collier Books, 1962), pp. 123-24.

3. "*vihitatvāccāśramakarmāpi*" (and duties of the *Āśrama* are to be performed), and again "*sahakāritvena ca*" (duties are to be performed as a means to knowledge. Cf. Swami Visveswaranand, ed., *Brahma-sūtras* (Mayavati, Almora: Advaita Ashrama, 1948), pp. 434-35. But here it should be noted that these actions are not for the attainment of *svarga* (heaven).

Our awareness of God as Lord, lifts our spiritual life above the worldly life. God for Śaṁkara is at the same time a savior God; the saving knowledge comes through his grace. This theological basis of the Advaita Vedānta implies the abjuration of the ego-centric will. The will of man, in the terminology of the Gītā is to be a sacrifice in the will of God.[1] In the denial of the self-will based on the metaphysical conviction of God as *antaryāmin* (immanent) raises the seeker above the perplexities and anxieties of life. This ideal looks to be negative at its face value but it aims at the realization of the company of God in the scheme of spiritual life.[2]

Here it might be asked whether the denial of self-will and dedication of everything to God might mean indifference to action. But it has been made very clear by the *Gītā* and the *Vedānta*, as we pointed out earlier that one must perform one's allotted work but renounce its fruits. In other words, one must remain detached and do one's work. Renunciation of fruit does not mean indifference to the result of action as it is based on the promise from God that "He who renounces reaps a thousand-fold" or "*na me bhaktaḥ praṇaśyati*" (my devotee will stand protected).[3]

Having shown the status and the purpose of *Īśvara* in the Advaita Vedānta from *taṭastha* point of view, we shall examine the nature of the world which is a fact that no body can deny. We will also see the meaning of renunciation pertaining to the world. To begin with, the world is beginningless in time.[4] A beautiful hymn of the *Ṛgveda* confirms the above.

Who knows for certain? Who shall here declare it? Whence was it born, and whence came this creation? The gods were

---

1. *mayi sarvāṇi karmāṇi saṁnyasyādhyātmacetasā, nirāśīrnirmamo bhūtvā, yuddhyasva vigatjvaraḥ. Ye me matamidaṁ nityamanutiṣṭhanti mānavāḥ, śraddhāvanto'nasūyanto mucyante te'pi karmabhiḥ. Gītā*, Ch. III. 30-31.
Radhakrishnan, *The Bhagavadgītā*, pp. 144-45.

2. *matkarmakṛnmatparamo madbhaktaḥ saṅgavarjitaḥ,*
nirvairaḥ sarvabhūteṣu yaḥ sa māmeti pāṇḍava. Gītā XI-55.

3. See Mahadev Desai, ed., *The Gospel of Selfless Action or the Gītā According to Gandhi* (Ahmedabad, 1946), pp. 120-128.

4. *na karmāvibhāgād iti cennānāditvāt; upapadyati cāpy upalabhyati ca.* See Radhakrishnan, *The Brahma-sūtras*, p. 364.

born after this world's creation : then who can know from whence it has arisen; and whether he has or has not produced it: he who surveys it in the highest heaven He only knows, or perhaps even he may not know.[1]

In its acceptance of the beginninglessness of the world along with the eternal *Īśvara*, the *Vedānta* has safeguarded not only the purity of *Īśvara* but also the responsibility of the *jīvas*. The *jīvas* have been freed from the limitations of fatalism or predestination. They are responsible for their actions and nothing but their actions. This position also affirms that the world is not the creation of the human mind. It has its own status. It is on this account that Śaṁkara has attacked the *Vijñānavādins* (Buddhist idealists) who denied the existence of the external objects independent of a beginningless stream of cognitions.[2] The empirical world of objects is again differentiated from the dream objects (*Prātibhāsika satya*). Only the latter is sublated in the waking experience and not the objects of the empirical world.[3] These arguments suffice to show that Śaṁkara does not deny the existence of the empirical world, contrary to common opinion. The world has been accepted as providing opportunities for the spiritual fulfilment through the four ends of life (*catvāri puruṣārathāni*), viz., *dharma*, *artha*, *kāma* and *mokṣa*. It is a world, as said by one of the *Upaniṣads*, which arose from bliss, is sustained by bliss and is destined to return to bliss.[4] The world has been compared by the *Gītā* with the

---

1. S. Radhakrishnan and Charles A. Moore, eds., *A Source Book in Indian Philosophy* (Princeton: Princeton University Press, 1917), pp. 23-24.

2. Śaṁkara criticizes on the following grounds:
Upalabhyate hi pratipratyayaṁ bāhyo'rthaḥ stambhaḥ kuḍyam, ghaṭaḥ paṭa iti (the eternal thing cannot be denied as it is cognized in every act of knowledge). —*Vedānta Sūtras* II.ii.28.
Upalabdhivyatireko'pi balād arthasyābhyupagantavyaḥ upalabdher eva. nahi kaścid upalabdhim eva stambhaḥ kuḍyaṁ cety upalabhate. Upalabdhiviṣaytvenaiva tu stambha-kuḍyādīn sarve laukikā upalabhante (the cognizing act cannot be the object cognized and how can a comparison be made with an object which is non-existent). *Ibid.*, see also II.ii.29.

3. *Ibid.*, II. 2, 28-29.

4. *ānando brahmeti vyajānāt, ānandādd hy eva khalv imāni bhūtāni jāyante, ānandena jātāni jīvanti, ānandaṁ prayanty abhisaṁviśanti.* —*Tai. Up.* III. 6.1.

eternal *aśvattha* whose roots are above and branches below.[1] A.G. Krishnawarrier explains the advaitic implication of this point: "The aim of Advaita Vedānta is to point the way upwards. Thus this world which seems to divide us from God will appear as the bridge which connects and gives a passage into him. Forming the *taṭasthalkaṣaṇa* of *Brahman*, the world in *Advaita* fulfils its sole purpose by awakening us to the truth that is *Brahman*."[2]

In the light of the above discussion, we can further substantiate the view, we referred to earlier that *avidyā* (with which the world has been equated) is not unreal in the ordinary sense of the term. Here the word "*avidyā*" does not stand for its complete negation or denial (*asat*) or '*sat*' (Reality) but being opposite of knowledge, it is indescribable (*anirvacaniya*).[3] Put simply, whatever truth the world has is because of *Brahman* : It does not have any substantial status independently of *Brahman*.[4] *Avidyā* as opposite of knowledge, is founded in the

---

1. *Ūrdhvamūlamadhaḥ śākhamaśvattham prāhuravyayam,*
chandāṁsi yasya parṇāni yastam veda sa vedavit. *Gītā*, XV. 1.

J.G. Arapura in his learned article "The Upside Down Tree of the Bhagavadgītā" Ch. XV, *Numen*, Vol. XXVII (forthcoming, April, 1975) draws the following conclusion from the *aśvattha* tree of the *Gītā*: (1) "The Upside-down tree is no new innovation, its inverted position having been there from the genesis of the concept in the Vedas as representing no doubt, clear anticipation of an ontology of the cosmos (rather than cosmology), re-appearing in the *Gītā*, the *Kaṭha* and the *Mahābhārata* (*Anugītā*), expressing essentially what has been vastly more elaborately set forth in the *Vedānta* philosophy in subsequent times. (2) The ontology of the cosmos is something which goes hand in hand with a particular kind of self-knowledge, a wisdom by means of which as a sword is alone able to deal with the world: knowledge is also detachment—hence *asaṅgaśastreṇa dṛḍhena* (*Gītā*) or *Jñānena paramāsinā* (*anugītā*).

2. A. G. Krishnawarrier, *The Concept of Mukti in Advaita Vedānta* (Madras: University of Madras, 1961), p. 370.

3. *apahnavavacano' nirvacanīyatāvacanaśca. Ibid.*, p. 380.

4. T.R.V. Murti states: "This position means that in every experience there is the real thing-in-itself, which is given; it serves as the passive substratum for the superimposition of thought-categories (i.e., difference, change, particularity). The empirical world of appearance is real, but as Brahman. . . only the knowledge of Brahman is pure knowledge." See Murti, *The Central Philosophy of Buddhism*, p. 315.

Brahman, the only real, the Real of the Real (*satyasya satyam*) and therefore it cannot be completely a false knowledge. The experienced world of phenomena which for any philosophical or religious system cannot remain unexplained, can only be explained not by explaining it away as false knowledge but establishing its status in the structure of *Jñāna*. The Advaita Vedānta is not an exception to it. The recognition of *Brahman* in the form of *Īśvara* from the *taṭasthalakṣaṇa* has been posited by Śaṁkara to overcome the above impasse.[1] The full significance of this position becomes very clear when we accept the Advaitic position that God is Real in relation to the phenomenal world. The Reality of God is itself in danger when the phenomenal world is discarded as *avidyā* in the sense of being false. The realization of *Brahman* progresses from truth to truth or from the lesser truth to the higher truth. The phenomenal world, if taken to be false (*mithyā*) in the ordinary sense of the term, cannot point to God. It points to God in order to transcend its limitations which are real and in need of removal. This cannot be explained by taking the world as false. The world is not negated even at the stage of the God-directed will and God-centred love. It is in this sense that Śaṁkara declares that the personal love of God is the central theme of the *Gitā*.[2]

The same spirit runs in Śaṁkara's commentary where the realization of freedom has been attributed to the grace of God. The following verse of the *Gitā* is to be noted : "He who has known *Nārāyaṇa*, the receiver of all sacrifice and all penance, both as their instigator and their end, who benefits all beings without reward, who dwells in the beast and controls all works, and their fruits, who witnesses all thoughts—he attains *śānti*, the cessation of all *saṁsāra*."[3] The *Īśvara* of the *Gitā* explains

---

1. *Vedānta Sūtra*, 1.1.12; *Br. Up.*, II. 3.6, III. 8.8., IV. 5.15; *Ch. Up.*, 24.1, and *Tai. Up.* II. 3.6.

2. *nā'haṁ vedair na tapasā na dānena na ca 'jyayā, śakya evaṁvidho draṣṭuṁ dṛṣṭavān asi māṁ yathā. bhaktyā tv ananyayā śakya aham evaṁvidho 'rjuna, jñātum draṣṭum ca tattvena praveṣṭuṁ ca paraṁtapa.* *Gitā*, XI, 53-54. Radhakrishnan, *The Bhagavadgītā*, pp. 288-289.

3. *Ibid.*, 294-95.

and justifies religion and the morality of *svadharma*. This religion directly leads to liberation as it is conducive to purity of the mind (*sattva-śuddhi*).[1]

The underlying spirit of renunciation does not call for the giving up of the empirical world altogether. Rather it certainly rests on a kind of harmonious relationship between the empirical world and the spiritual reality without which it loses its significance. Philosophy, for the Advaitins, is an attempt to look at things not as they appear, but as they really are; it is an elaborate explanation of the relationship between ultimate reality and the phenomenal world. The world has been treated not apart from reality but along with reality, viewed either from the *svarūpalakṣaṇa* or *taṭasthalakṣaṇa*. Renunciation does not imply a mere escape from the world as it would defeat the very ideal of Vedāntic philosophy. What is most important here to note is not the value or significance of the world *per se* but the self-culture and spiritual insight of the renunciants who look at things. Renunciation, in its ultimate analysis, is an attitude or better, an enlightened attitude which helps man to face the world without exhausting himself within the world. A renunciant does not cease to act but all the activities remain as it were cancelled in his relation to the unbroken awareness of integral experience. In other words, the world stands renounced as different from the vision of self; it cannot catch hold of him or delude him.[2] Here the gulf between the phenomenal world and the ground it embodies is abolished; the world is truth as *Brahman* has come to realization.[3] The renunciant functions in the temporal world with the consciousness of a timeless infinite. "He has *trikāladṛṣṭi*, an intuition of time in which past, present and future exist together in the self-knowledge and self-power of the Eternal. He is no more a victim of time.[4]

1. *brahmaṇyādhāya karmāṇi saṁgaṁ tyaktvā karoti yaḥ,*
lipyate na sa pāpena padmapatramivāmbhasā.
(He who does actions, offering them to Brahman, abandoning attachment, is not tainted by sin as a lotus leaf by water). — *Gītā* V. 10.

2. R.B. Singh, *The Vedānta of Śaṁkara* (Jaipur : Bharat Publishing House, 1949), pp. 293-94.

3. S. Radhakrishnan, *Great Indians* (Bombay: Hind Kitabs, 1949), p. 88.

4. Janaka and Aśvapati have been mentioned as the knowers of the Self in the *Bṛ. Up.* (III. 1.1) and *Ch. Up.* (V. II.5).

On the basis of what we have said above, renunciation does not exclude a life of activity for others' purposes. Śaṁkara, for example, has clearly admitted that the *jñānin* (renunciant) may engage in actions for the purpose of teaching other, having no purpose to be attained for himself.[1] Vidyāraṇya also states that an enlightened person can work for others (*parecchā*).[2] But it is a fact that there are several references in the *Vedānta* which clearly assert the irreconcilability between *karma* and *saṁnyāsa.* The present section will deal with the metaphysical structure of this issue.

Karma, Jñāna and Saṁnyāsa

The main emphasis of the Vedas was on *Karma* although evidences of the importance attached to asceticism and renunciation are implicit there. The *Karma-Mīmāṁsakas* pursue the philosophy of action further and take it to be the main purport of the Vedas.[3] The term '*karma*' is primarily used for sacrifice but in a general sense it includes all actions, physical or mental, but for the Vedāntins, mental actions such as meditation (*dhyāna*) and reflection (*vicāra*) are to be excluded from the list of *karmas.* They prescribe only those mental actions in the *vividiṣā saṁnyāsa* (renunciation of the seeker) and exclude other actions. But even Śaṁkara accepts the purificatory function of *karmas* without which the spiritual attainment is regarded as impossible.[4] The *Vedānta* does not go further than that, but restricts the role of *karma* to the purificatory level.[5] The reason why *karma* has been excluded from the higher level of knowledge by the Vedāntins is its incompatability with *Jñāna*. *Jñāna* means

1. *svaprayojanābhāvāt lokasaṁgrahārtham pūrvavat karmaṇi pravṛtto'pi. Śaṁkara's Commentary on Bhagavadgītā*, IV, 20.

2. See Hari Prasad Sastri, *Pañcadaśī*, p. 37.

3. A. B. Keith, *The Karma-Mīmāṁsā* (London, Calcutta, 1921), p. 5.

4. *na hi acalato śuddhirasti—Bhāṣya* on *Ch. Up.* See Brahma, *Hindu Sadhana*, p. 91.

5. *vividiṣuḥ khalu yukta ekāgratayā śravaṇamanane kartumutsahate, tato 'sya tattvamasīti vākyānnirvicikitsajñānamutpadyate. na ca nirvicikitsam tattvamasīti vākyārthamavadhārayataḥ karmaṇyadhikāro'sti yena bhāvanāyām vā bhāvanākārye vā sākṣātkāra karmaṇāmupayogaḥ Etena vṛttir ūpasākṣātkārakārya 'pavargekarmaṇāmupayogo dūrānnirasto veditavyaḥ. Bhāmatī*, III, 4, 27.

tattvajñāna which is opposed to action because the latter cannot function independently of the world of multiplicities or the realm of ignorance. But here again Śaṁkara excludes only those actions which are brought about by desires of fruits and not bodily activities. If this interpretation is correct, Śaṁkara stands for advocating *karmas* for the purification of the mind which once accomplished with the dawn of metaphysical knowledge, desire-impelled actions automatically stop and man at this stage performs virtuous action by his nature. Put in other words, *Jñāna* and *Karmas* are compatible before the realization of *Jñāna* even according to Śaṁkara and when *Jñāna* has been reached, the enlightened person becomes example for the society and lives a life of self-denial or complete asceticism which does not have its root in action but in metaphysical knowledge. Śaṁkara indirectly hints at this idea,[1] although its development takes place in the *Gitā* which propounds the culmination of action in knowledge where action is not negated but enriched and ennobled.[2] In the absence of such an understanding, the whole positive implication of the *Iśvara* ideal in the *Vedānta* falls to the ground and Śaṁkara would have no justification for forwarding a case for the *avatāra* (incarnation) or even the *Jivanmukta*. Vidyāraṇya in his *Jivanmuktiviveka* explicitly asserts that *Jñāna* does not dispel all actions : "It is not to be thought, however, that for a person whose mind is free from all desires, all actions must cease, nor that the operations of the bodily organs such as the eyes, etc. or mental operations need be absent.[3] All that Śaṁkara meant by the incompatibility between *Jñāna* and *Karma* was simply that once a person is enlightened all the limitations of the *karmas* which divide oneself from the rest of mankind are burnt to ashes and *karmas* are reduced to actions in

1. *apekṣate ca vidyā sarvāṇyāśramakarmāṇi nātyantamanapekṣaiva . . utpannā hi vidyā phalasiddhiṁ prati na kiñcidanyadapekṣati utpattiṁ prati tu apekṣate.* —*Brahmasūtra Śāṁkarabhāṣya*, III. 4.26.

2. *Gatasaṅgasya muktasya jñānāvasthitacetasaḥ,*
yajñāyācarataḥ karma samagraṁ pravilīyate. —*Gītā* IV. 23.

Also, *tadviddhi praṇipātena paripraśnena sevayā,*
upadekṣyanti te jñānam jñāninastattvadarśinaḥ. —*Gītā*. IV. 34.

3. *na ca nirvāsanāmanaskasya jīvanahetuvyavahāro lupyeteti śaṅkanīyaṁ kiṁ cakṣurādivyavahārasya lopaḥ kiṁ vā mānasavyavahārasya.* Vidyāraṇya, *Jīvanmuktiviveka*, p. 79.

the ordinary narrow sense. In fact, in his commentary on the *Gītā*, he clearly affirms this when he says that "a *Jñānin* does nothing, even doing everything because of his realization of the Self as non-doer."[1] This spirit of egolessness, as we asserted earlier, is the characteristic of renunciation.

The actions of the *Jñānin*, Śaṁkara rightly holds, is not of the ordinary type because every action suffers with one or another kind of egoism. It is absolutely unmotivated action which springs from inner realization. It is impossible to make a judgment about it on the purely psychological level of existence, where ordinary morality reigns. Only in this sense, renunciation transcends morality. Once a person has perfected himself, he becomes his own light and transcends all the injunctions of the scriptures.[2]

Nothing remains to be satisfied after realising Brahman. The significance of moral and spiritual discipline aims at actual realization of the immediate experience of the unity of existence which can only be attained by transcending our actual experience of difference and multiplicity. Since the Absolute is devoid of distinctions whether homogeneous (*sajātīya*), heterogeneous (*vijātīya*) or inherent (*svagata*), the spiritual life is total, integral and undivided life and yet devoid of anxiety whether of a practical or religious nature. In the pursuit of pure *Brahman* one is summoned to go beyond even *Īśvara*, precisely because *Īśvara* himself, as personal God, is nevertheless the transcendental and universal Ego although that hypothesis is due to his being the cosmic manifestation of pure *Brahman*. This is the

---

1. *tyaktvā karmaphalāsaṅgaṁ nityatṛpto nirāśrayaḥ, karmaṇyabhipravṛtto'pi naiva kiñcit karoti saḥ.* (*niṣkriyātmadarśanasampannatvāt naiva kiñcit karoti saḥ*). —*Gītā* IV. 20.
also, Madhusūdana Sarasvatī commenting on the *Gītā*, V. 8, also holds the same view when he says: *Yasmāt sarvavyāpāreṣvapyātmano kartṛtvameva paśyati ataḥ kurvannapi na lipyate iti yuktamevoktam.* —Brahma, *Hindu Sadhana*, p. 103.

2. *avidyāvadviṣayāṇyeva pratyakṣādīni pramāṇāni śāstrāṇi ceti.* Introduction to Śaṁkara's Comm. on the *Brahma-Sūtra.*

yāvaddehātmavijñānaṁ bādhyate na pramāṇataḥ, prāmāṇyam karmaśāstrāṇām tāvadevopalabhyate. quoted from N. K. Brahma, *Hindu Sadhana*, p. 114.

stage "beyond good and evil" Rudolf Otto beautifully presents it in the following paragraph :

> When I came out of God, that is, into multiplicity then all things proclaimed : "There is a God" (the personal God, creator or things). Now this cannot make me blessed, for hereby I realize myself as creature (*Kārya, Kāladeśanimitta*). But in the breaking through (i.e., through all limitations, in *samyagdarśanaṁ*) I am more than all creatures, I am neither God nor creature : I am that which, I was and shall remain, now and for evermore, (the *ātman* as *nityamukta* and *nityasiddha*). There I receive a thrust which carries me above all angels (as the *mukta* is above all *devas* and their heavens). By this sudden thrust I become so sick that God (*Īśvāra*) is not sufficient for me, so far as he is only God and all His divine works. For in this breaking through I perceive that God and I are in common. There I am what I was. There I neither increase nor decrease. . .there God is received into the soul.[1]

It appears to us that any attempt to show the irreconciliability between *Karma* and *Jñāna* is futile and as we have shown earlier that Śaṁkara has been unfortunately greatly misunderstood with regard to this problem. It should be clearly understood, however, that Śaṁkara was himself a great *Karmayogin* and it seems to be inconsistent to hold that *Jñāna* dispels action. In fact, the *Jñānin* has greater responsibility towards society and its obligations than ignorant people. Moreover, if the world forms no 'other' to *Brahman*, a complete withdrawal from the world is not understandable. If the world were 'other' from *Brahman* in the state of *Jñāna* as is the case with the *Sāṁkhya*, a life of, inactivity or escapism might be justified. Therefore, it seems right to hold that when Śaṁkara talks about the diametrically opposed nature of *Jñāna* and *Karma*, he implies only those *Karmas* which are not backed by *Jñāna*. Since the *Jñāna* transforms the whole perspective of man, reality and the universe, the *Karmas* should not be excluded from this enormous transformation. At the stage of enlightenment, everything remains as they are except the

1. Otto, *Mysticism*, pp. 31-32.

attitude of man which constitutes his philosophy or, broadly speaking, his way of life.

Secondly, if the *Vedānta* holds the doctrine of cosmic purpose which *Īśvara* himself serves, there is no inconsistency in regarding the *Jivanmuktas* to serve the cosmic purpose without their interest being involved in such a purpose. Even those schools of thought, i.e., the *Viśiṣṭādvaita* of Rāmānuja and the *Nyāya-Vaiśeṣika* which do not accept the ideal of the *Jīvanmukta*, have accepted the role of the enlightened person in the cosmic purpose.[1] It seems to be unjustified to hold that the *Vedānta* can deny such a role. It is from this standpoint that the Gītā says : "He who finds *karma* in *akarma*, and *akarma* in *karma*, is intelligent and united to the Divine, and the doer of all actions."[2]

The problem regarding the status of the *Karma*, *Jñāna* and *Saṁnyāsa* have evoked a good deal of controversy in the history of Indian thought. It is not an easy task to arrive at a general conclusion regarding their status. In the light of what we have said, however, it might be emphasized that *Brahman*, when viewed from the empirical point of view, *sub specie temporis*, will encourage the cultivation of all those values which are necessary for the spiritual progress of man. But to reach the absolute truth, the *Jñānayoga* has been recognized the path par excellence, which has also been regarded as *saṁnyāsa-mārga*. The *Jñāna-mārga* or *Saṁnyāsamārga* represents the philosophical ideal of the *Vedānta* whereas the former where *Īśvara* reigns supreme is the religious ideal. These two ideals are not opposed to each other. They should be taken as supplementary. What the ideal of *Brahman* at the cosmic or empirical level accomplishes, the same is the case with *Brahman* at the acosmic or transcendental level. Both uplift the motive beyond the ordinary calculation of

---

1. Rāmānuja accepts the need for renunciation and self-suppression whatever course of discipline a man may follow. It is not belief in permanent self that matters in service but eradication of selfishness which is the enemy of true life.

2. *karmaṇyakarma yaḥ paśyed akarmaṇi ca karma yaḥ, sa buddhimān manuṣyeṣu sa yuktaḥ kṛtsnakarmakṛt.* —*Gītā*, IV. 18.

interests and in this sense are renunciatory in their perspectives. Both are not opposed to action except that for the former, action is based on devotion or dedication to God and also to the world-solidarity, which are the explicit purpose of God, while for the latter action is transformed into knowledge resulting in the complete transformation of man to such an extent that he becomes virtuous by nature.

Chapter Four

PERSONAL DIMENSION OF RENUNCIATION

Meaning and Significance

In this chapter we will concentrate on the personal dimension of renunciation which constitutes the climax of spiritual consciousness. The study of the Vedānta is based on, and directed primarily to, the understanding of the absolute freedom. It can only be accomplished by being devoid of all passions which constitute human conditioning. As has been observed before, the secret of self-knowledge consists in becoming aware of absolute freedom which is also being indicated by other *Sādhanas* (discipline) like *Karmayoga*, *bhaktiyoga* etc. If self-knowledge represents the personal dimension of renunciation, it should not be understood, however, that it does not have any implication for the cosmic purpose. The *Vedānta* in so far as it is rooted in the Vedas has altogether a different message and can deal with it more positively on the metaphysical foundation of *Brahman*. The personal dimension of renunciation simply shows the self-perfection of the *sādhaka* himself, which is a fundamental requisite for being of any service to mankind. The discipline of self-knowledge through renunciation, however, serves the purpose of man's freeing himself from the superficialities of life (life at its surface value) by being spiritually aware of Reality concealed in the phenomenal world demanding to be known. This consciousness which is termed 'religious' is central to the understanding of Indian philosophy of life and views on life not only after death but even at a time when man is yet alive. The nature of man as understood and believed in this context of religious consciousness having its bearings on the spiritual living of a man in Indian society in general and in an age of that society in particular is what we call the personal dimension of renunciation. The full-fledged theory of the subtle elements of the term 'personal' used in modern scholarship in a specific way is not applicable to our use of the term, the few glimmerings of which we find in the *Upaniṣads*.[1]

The richness of the Vedāntic speculation on this question has no doubt been due to the persistent belief of Indian philosophers that a correct knowledge of the 'person' or 'personal' provides only remedy for anxieties and sufferings of human existence. Self-knowledge, accordingly, occupied the highest place in such a scheme of thinking. J.G. Arapura while discussing the real purpose of a comparative study of religion has emphasized the importance of this topic: "It is clear", he remarks, "that nothing partial, piecemeal or occasional could serve this goal. If religion is considered just a phenomenon among phenomena then it would hardly warrant philosophical study. As the call of philosophy is to study necessary rather than accidental things, religion has to be so interpreted as to fall within the former category, and it will automatically do so if its indispensibility for self-knowledge can be demonstrated".[2]

The personal dimension of renunciation consists in the indispensibility of 'self-knowledge'. The profounder the realization of this 'self-knowledge', the deeper is its significance for the correct appreciation of what Arapura calls the "Indian sphere of spirit." Of all the subjects of philosophical discourses that have occupied the Indian mind, that of the self-knowledge along with renunciation occupies the most prominent place. Political organizations, social institutions, religio-ethical life, all have been reflected upon with this perspective which in its turn has passed through certain adjustments in order to make itself more suited to the understanding of the multifarious

1. *na tatra cakṣur gacchati na vāg gacchati no manaḥ,*
na vidmo na vijānīmo yathaitad anuśisyāt. —*Kena Up*. 1.3.

(There the eye goes not, speech goes not, nor the mind; we know not, we understand not, how one can teach this). See Radhakrishnan, *The Principal Upanisads* p. 582. Also *na dṛṣṭer draṣṭāram paśyeḥ na śruter śrotāraṁ śṛṇuyāḥ, na mater mantāraṁ manvīthāh na vijñātāram vijānīyāḥ eṣa ta ātmā sarvāntaraḥ ato' nyad ārtam. Bṛ. Up*., III. 4.2. (You cannot see the seer of seeing, you cannot hear the hearer of hearing, you cannot think the thinker of thinking, you cannot understand the understander of understanding. He is your self which is in all things. Everything else is of evil).

Ibid., p. 220.

2. Arapura, *Religion as Anxiety and Tranquillity*, p. 7.

aspects of complex civilization throughout the Indian philosophical development.

It is an undeniable fact that the emphasis on the personal dimension of spiritual experience has been central to Indian thought but some of the systems have falsely taken it for the acquisition of supernatural powers.[1] This phenomenon might constitute an interesting topic for discussion especially with reference to renunciation but it has been excluded simply because it cannot strictly be called 'spiritual' or 'personal' and hence condemned by the Buddha, Patañjali, Śaṁkara and Ramakrishna.[2] Vidyāraṇya, the author of the *Jivan-Mukti-Viveka* condemns the occult powers attained by renunciants and appreciates the knowers of the *Brahman*:

> The mind of one who has attained *gnosis*, does not attach itself to any particular thing; for, ever content and with his self in a state of supreme tranquillity, he rests himself in the Ātman alone. Wonders, such as floating in the air, have often been performed by persons, who have acquired remarkable powers by the practice of incantations, penance and trance! What is there extraordinary in them? There is only one special feature to be noticed in the man of *gnosis*, which he does not share in common with ignorant men, viz., a detached and pure mind, due to the giving up of desire in all things whatever.[3]

1. Such as *Haṭha-yoga-pradīpikā* and various *tāntric* techniques like *ṣaṭ-cakranirūpaṇa* and *pāduka-pañcaka* and cases like *piśācasiddhi* and *vetālasiddhi*, all lay emphasis on the supernatural powers. The powers attained through *tapas* and various ascetic exercises have been recognized in the Veda but in the *Upaniṣads* and the Advaita Vedānta they are absent to a large extent.

2. *Yoga-Sūtra*, II, 15-55: "By giving up even these powers comes the destruction of the very seed of evil which leads to *Kaivalya*. The saving knowledge is that knowledge of discrimination which simultaneously covers all objects, in all their variations." See G. N. Jha, trans., *Yoga-darsan* (Bombay: Theosophical Publication, 1907). "But in the case of one who practises the best course of the discipline of devotion to me obtains my grace, these attainments are mere obstacles and waste of time." *Gītā*, XV. 13. "Beware of these powers and desire them not... for occult powers increase man's egotism and this makes him forgetful of God." F. Maxmüller, *Rāmakrishna: His Life and Saying* (Calcutta: Advaita Ashrama, 1951), pp. 129-30.

3. *Jñasya kaśmiṁścidapyeṣā bhavatyatiśaye na dhīḥ,*
nityatṛptaḥ praśāntātmā sa ātmanyeva tiṣṭhati.
mantrasiddhaistapassiddhairyogasiddhaiśca bhūriśaḥ,
kṛtamākāsayānādi tatra kā syādapūrvatā.
eka eva viśeṣo' sya na samo mūḍhabuddhibhiḥ
sarvatrāsthāparityāgānnirāgamanalam manaḥ. —*Jīvan-Mukti-Viveka*, p. 142.

The *Dhammapada*, likewise, lays great emphasis on the religious experience, the steadiness of thought, tranquillity of mind and perfect knowledge.[1]

Therefore the problem which needs investigation is not the acquisition of the occult powers but the life of the renunciants who are established in *Brahman*. Knowledge (*Jñāna*) and renunciation (*saṁnyāsa*) are complementary in the sense that *Jñāna* which is needed for the realization of ultimate goal in life culminates in direct practical life of renunciation. It is on this account that Śaṁkara regards only the *Jñānin* to be a *saṁnyāsin*. The attainment of the goal of life, according to Śaṁkara, signifies nothing more than perfecting the means to it. That is to say that the end here is not external to the means but is only the means stabilized.[2] Pointing out the significance of the identity between *Jñāna* and *saṁnyāsa*, which we have discussed earlier, M. Hiriyanna remarks :

> This gives us a clue as regards the kind of life which a knower leads and enables us thereby to grasp the exact meaning of *mokṣa*. We have mentioned two aids to the attainment of the goal. Pursuing the good and acquiring the knowledge of true self. Corresponding to these the life of the knower, broadly speaking, will be characterized by two features. In the first place, it will be entirely free from the tyranny of the egoistic self, and therefore also free from the feverish activity for gratifying personal desires, which can never be completely gratified. In the second place it will be marked by an unshakable conviction in the unity of all, and consequently by love for others—love for them not as equals but as essentially one with oneself.[3]

---

1. F. Maxmüller, ed. and trans., The *Dhammapada* (Delhi: Motilal Banarsidass, 1968), pp. 23-30.

2. In his commentary on the *Gītā*, Śaṁkara says that immediate freedom accrues to those renunciants who have attained the *samyagdarśana*. *Samyagdarśananiṣṭhānām sannyāsinām sadyomuktiruktā*. See *The Bhagavad-Gītā*, p. 163.

3. M. Hiriyanna, "Philosophy of Values", in Haridas Bhattacharya, ed., *The Cultural Heritage of India* (Calcutta : The Ramakrishna Mission, 1969), II, 652-653.

The link between *Jñāna* and *saṁnyāsa* in the Vedāntic tradition attains its complete maturity in the life of the *Jīvanmukta* (those who are liberated in this life). Before we deal with the ideal of the *Jīvanmukti,* one point must be clarified here. The personal dimension of renunciation is different from the devotional dimension of renunciation. The former culminates in the liberation here and now whereas the latter believes in the *Videha-mukti* (liberation after death).

Personal and Devotional Contrasted

As we have noticed in the monistic system of thought, it is the realization of the identity between the personal or individual self and the ultimate self or *Brahman* that constitutes liberation. The devotional aspect of renunciation, no doubt, covers the freedom from egotism (*ahaṁkāra*) in one's complete dedication to *Īśvara* as supreme reality but its transformation into the service of *Īśvara* (*Kaiṅkarya*) and also humanity, makes *Īśvara* and humanity exterior to oneself.[1] The *Viśiṣṭādvaita* (qualified monism) of Rāmānuja attaches so much importance to *prapatti* (self-surrender) that it seems essential even at the final stage. The Advaita Vedānta accepts the loving or devotional contemplation of *Īśvara* but at a preparatory stage and not at the final stage simply because the distinction between the Lord and creature which is unsurmountable in the *Viśiṣṭādvaita* stands as an obstacle in the ideal of unity. This distinction would result in a freedom in the hypothetical hereafter as this distinction can never be annulled, making the ideal of *Jīvanmukti* impossible. At the *pāramārthika* (transcendental) level, the *Vedānta* cannot tolerate any distinction, even the distinction between existence and knowledge, implied by discursive thought. The theory of self-suppression on the part of the *bhakta* (devotee) in the *Viśiṣṭādvaita* is quite understandable but by adding another personality to Reality to which the devotee is subservient as a creature, it creates an unbridgeable gulf between the two. Liberation for such a system of thought can only be described in terms of divine vision and experience of God which is not believed to arise until after the end of life.

1. For details see C.D. Sharma, *Indian Philosophy : A Critical Survey*, (American ed : Barnes and Noble Inc., 1962), pp. 355-359.

Man's aim, according to the *Vedānta*, is not attainment of the ideal outside the scope of his present life but as one of the *Upaniṣads* beautifully puts it, "when all the desires the heart harbours are gone, man becomes immortal and reaches *Brahman* here."[1] But here it should be remembered that even those systems of thought which do not believe in the *Jīvanmukti* ideal, clearly recognize the possibility of complete transformation of man's attitude towards the world which can be attained within this life. According to all of them, the evils and sufferings linked with *saṁsāra* carry with them the seeds of their own destruction; they exist only for those who are ignorant not only of the real but also of the good. R.P. Singh has maintained this position very strongly and thinks that the traditional assessment of Śaṁkara's philosophy fails to do it full justice precisely because it has ignored "the great truth that Śaṁkara's is a philosophy of values primarily and not an existential system. He concerns himself with the problem of Appearance and Reality only to bring out the value side of the universe. For him the truth of the universe is constituted by the value it possesses."[2] The world is the appearance of *Brahman*. Whatever reality the world has is derived from *Brahman*. When isolated from *Brahman*, it becomes false. The finite individual is to be in constant touch with the infinite and thus to live not the isolated existence. This partaking of the Infinite is what we mean by the word 'personal dimension', called *Brahmasadbhāva* (existing in *Brahman*) or *Brahmasaṁstha*.[3] The *Vedāntaparibhāṣā* of Dharmarāja puts it like this : "Thus, therefore, release results from Brahman-knowledge; and that (release) consists in the removal of evil and the attainment of the unsurpassable Brahman-bliss; hence is established that fruit."[4] The central motif of

1. *Yadā sarve pramucyante kāmā ye'sya hṛdi śritāḥ,*
atha martyo'mṛto bhavati atra brahma samaśnute. *Kaṭha Up.* II.3.14.

2. Singh, *The Vedānta of Śaṁkara*, p. 11.

3. *Uttamo brahmasadbhāvaḥ dhyānabhāvastu madhyamaḥ,*
stutirjapo'dhamo bhāvo bahiḥpūjādhamādhamā. *Mahānirvāṇa Tantra*, XIV, 122.

4. *tadevaṁ brahmajñānānmokṣaḥ sa cānarthanivṛttirniratiśayabrahmānandāvāptiśca iti siddham prayojanam.* *Vedāntaparibhāṣā* IX.56.

the Upaniṣads lies in the discovery of *Ātman* and the method prescribed for the realization of *Ātman* not only as the real but also the good. Everything is good because of the Self: "Verily, not for the sake of the husband is the husband dear but for the sake of the self is the husband dear. Verily, not for the sake of the wife is the wife dear but for the sake of the self is the wife dear . . . verily, the Self, Maitreyi, is to be seen, to be heard, to be reflected on, to be meditated upon; when, verily the Self is seen, heard, reflected on and known, then all this is known."[1] For the matter under discussion, references could be made to the story of Virocana and Indra in the *Chāndogya*, the dialogue between Ajātaśatru and Bālāki in the *Bṛhadāraṇyaka*, the conversation between Sanatkumāra and Nārada in the *Chāndogya* and Naciketa and Yama in the *Kaṭha*. The approach in these *Upaniṣads* is completely personal not in the ordinary or psychological sense but in the sense of renunciation in terms of transcending the mind and its limitations in order to reach the innermost (*antarhṛdaya*) reality.

The state of *Brahman* is higher than mind (*manas*). No amount of psychological or intellectual equipment can enable us to apprehend the reality.[2] A clear distinction is drawn between *aparā* and *parā* vidyā. It is by becoming *manas* that *Brahman* transforms itself into the thought-activity. The purpose of the personal dimension of renunciation is to help the dawn of knowledge (*Jñāna*) by (a) the dissolution of the mind (*manonāśa*) and (b) the obliteration of latent desires (*vāsanākṣaya*).

The Dissolution of the Mind (*Manonāśa*)

By the term '*manonāśa*' is meant the cessation of the waves or modifications of the mind, called *citta-vṛttis*. It is the same as in Patañjali's *Yoga* system which gives the definition of *yoga* as *cittavṛttinirodhaḥ* (*yoga* as the suppression of the modifications of

1. *na vā are patyuḥ kāmāya patiḥ priyo bhavati, ātmanas tu kāmāya patiḥ priyo bhavati; na va are jāyāyai kāmāya jāyā priyā bhavati, ātmanas tu kāmāya jāyā priyā bhavati. . .ātmā vā are draṣṭavyaḥ śrotavyo mantavyo nididhyāsitavyaḥ maitreyi; ātmani khalv are dṛṣṭe, śrute, mate vijñāte, idam sarvam viditam.* —*Bṛ Up.* IV.5.6.
2. *naiṣā tarkeṇa matirāpaneyā*—*Kaṭha Up.*, 1.2.9.

mind).[1] M. Eliade divided these modalities of mind into three sections, namely, (a) errors and illusions (dreams, hallucinations, errors in perceptions, confusions etc.); (b) the sum total of normal psychological experience (everything felt, perceived or thought by the nonadept, by him who does not practise *yoga*); (c) the parapsychological experience brought out by the Yogic technique, and of course, accessible only to adepts.[2] The Advaitic position regarding the psychic apparatus is similar to the *Sāṁkhya-Yoga* except with the difference that unlike the latter, the psychic apparatus is dealt with as ultimately belonging to *Brahman*. The *Jiva* as designated by *antaḥkaraṇa* (internal sense organ), undergoing all empirical experiences within the psychophysical realm of existence, is nothing but *Brahman*, associated with *Upādhis* or adjuncts, due to which alone, *Brahman* appears as *Īśvara*, *Saṁsāra* and *Jiva*. The agency of the *Jiva* is accidental and not essential. And because it is linked with the modifications of the mind which presents thought in terms of thinker and doer, the agency is an act of superimposition, *adhyāsa*, on account of which he identifies himself with the doer. The idea of 'doer' (*kartā*) gives rise to egoism. The dissolution of the mind, in my judgment, has been prescribed by the Advaita Vedānta for freeing the mind from the egoism of being 'doer' (*kartā*) which creates a widespread gulf between rights and obligations, putting rights above the obligations by linking the former with the notion of the 'doer'. By making the individuality as simply provisional, the *Vedānta* transcends the limitations of egoism (*ahaṁkāra*). Here the consciousness of the obligations still continues but there is no awareness, whatsoever of one's rights. Once the conflict between rights and duties disappears, the renunciants still discharge their obligations but not at the plane of common morality. Buddhism accomplishes the same purpose by denying the idea of the individual self as permanent entity. The *Vedānta*, on the other hand, does not deny the provisional status of individuality but by including the dissolution of mind as one of the functions of renunciation, merges it finally in the Universal self.

1. *Yoga-sūtras*, 1.2. For details see J. H. Woods, *The Yoga System of Patañjali* (Massachusetts: Harvard Oriental Series, 1927), pp. 8-12.
2. Eliade, *Yoga*, p. 36.

Even those systems of thought which accept the independence or ultimacy of the individual self like the *Viśiṣṭādvaita*, Jainism and the *Nyāya-Vaiśeṣika*, do accept the denial of egoism. The denial of egoism, for the *Vedānta* serves a very positive ideal of life when it turns towards the fellowship of all living beings as oneself. The dissolution of the mind, therefore, should not be taken to imply passivity. The emphasis is laid on the cultivation of an attitude that gives rise to the discharge of one's obligations without the awareness of one's rights. Since the force of rights no longer acts, he has nothing to fear, for his acts no longer have any consequences for him. Only in this sense, the following statement of the *Taittirīya Upaniṣad* should be taken: "He is not troubled by thoughts like these: Have I not done the right? Have I done the wrong".[1] Such statements should not be taken in the sense of irresponsibility or negligence of duty.[2] Renunciation denies the assertion of rights but not devotion to duties. Renunciation is first and foremost an attitude and then anything else.

The Obliteration of Latent Desires (*Vāsanākṣaya*)

Latent desires of *vāsanās* here mean that which generate mental impressions, such as anger, jealousy, covetousness etc. As long as these *vāsanās* are not destroyed, the dissolution of mind (egoism) cannot take place. Latent desires have been explained as follows :

> Latent desires may be described as that hankering after things, which gain such mastery over the mind, as to preclude even enquiring into their antecedents and consequents. He at once becomes that which he identifies himself with, by force

1. *etaṁ he vā va na tapati, kiṁ ahaṁ sādhu nākaravam kiṁ ahaṁ pāpam akaravam iti.*—*Tai. Up.* II. 9-1.
2. *yogayukto viśuddhātmā vijitātmā jitendriyaḥ, sarvabhūtātmabhūtātmā kurvannapi na lipyate.*

(The Yogī who has cleansed himself, has gained mastery over his mind and all his senses, who has become one with the *Ātman* in all creation, although he acts he remains uneffected). See Desai, *The Gītā According to Gandhi*, p. 216.

> of strong and deep attachment and loses, O strong armed one ! memory of every other thing in the act. The man thus subdued by *vāsanā*, keeping his eye on anything whatever, is deluded into believing it as the real thing; owing to loss of control due to the powerful influence of *vāsanā*, the object (thus perceived) gives up its real form. Thus does one with beclouded eye, perceive everything quite in this deluded fashion, like one under the influence of a strong intoxicant.[1]

These *vāsanās* create tremendous difficulties for the renunciants. They are elusive in nature, difficult to control. In psychological terms, they may be regarded as constituting the subconscious which is difficult to extinguish.[2] Unless they are completely controlled, they always lead the *sādhaka* towards *phalatṛṣṇā* (thirst for fruits) and therefore to the egoistic direction. The *Vedānta* believes that the subconscious can be dominated by asceticism and conquered through metaphysical knowledge. One of the *smṛtis* describes the characteristic of an ascetic : "He is verily the typical ascetic, whose hands and feet are not restive, whose eyes and tongue are not restless; control of these is the true mark of an adept."[3] Pointing out another technique of controlling the *vāsanā*, the *Gitā* says : "Having restrained them all, he should sit harmonised, with Me as his supreme goal; for, whose senses are mastered, of him the understanding is well-poised. Therefore, O mighty armed ! Whose senses are all completely restrained from the objects of senses, of him the understanding is well-poised."[4] The control over *vāsanā* which can be accomplished through *Upāsanā* (devotion) as explained by the *Gitā*, can further be strengthened by turning to *Jñāna*—the highest form of *Upāsanā* : "What is there here ? What is It in Itself ? What is It made of ? Who are you ? Who am I ? What are these worlds ? Pray explain this to me at once." "All this is *Cit* (simple *Gnosis*) ; all this is *Cit* in itself; all this is made of

1. Sastri, *Jīvan-mukti-viveka of Vidyāraṇya*, p. 70.
2. *pūrvebhyastu prayatnebhyo viṣamo'yaṁ hi sanmataḥ, duḥsādho vāsanātyāgaḥ sumerūnmūlanādapi. Ibid.*, p. 48.
3. *na pāṇipādacapalo na netracapalo yatiḥ, na ca vākcapalaścaivamiti śiṣṭasya lakṣaṇaṁ. Ibid.*, p. 76.
4. *Bhagavad Gītā*, II. 60, 67.

Cit; thou art *Cit* and so am I; nay these worlds too are all *Cit*. In short the whole world is *Cit*."[1] It should not be thought, however, that one whose mind is devoid of all *vāsanās*, will have no connection with the world. Even Janaka is described as an enlightened person, who never ceased acting for the society. "I desire not what I have not; I care not to part from what I have; I stand in the Eternal Self in me; let that be mine, which has been mine." Thus taking thought, Janaka addressed himself, without the least attachment (to results), to whatever came up in the course of duty, even like the sun running his diurnal course. He relates himself not with the future, nor with what has gone by, he lives the present out with a smiling heart."[2]

If the obliteration of *vāsanās* is regarded as absolutely important for a *saṁnyāsin* in the *Vedānta*, it is for an ideal of a free life of a true *saṁnyāsin*. The *Jñāna* that is capable of effecting it should be a genuine mystical perception or self-knowledge (*sākṣāt-kāra*) based on the principle of one's identity with *Brahman*.

In a sense, it may be said here that the dissolution of the mind (*manonāśa*), obliteration of latent desires (*vāsanākṣaya*) and the dawn of *Jñāna* (*ātma-sākṣātkāra*) are not isolated spiritual techniques in the *Vedānta*. They constitute the whole spiritual life. The life of a renunciant is regarded as a life of enlightenment and complete perfection because of the removal of all the obstacles constituting the human bondage. In his commentary on the *Muṇḍaka Upaniṣad*, Śaṁkara regards the *Saṁnyāsin* as completely entitled to *Brahma-Jñāna* which yields *mokṣa*.[3] A

1. *Jīvan-mukti-viveka*, pp. 104-105.
2. *nābhivāñchāmyasaṁprāptaṁ saṁprāptaṁ na tyajāmyahaṁ,*
svastha ātmani tiṣṭhāmi yanmamāsti tadastu me.
iti sañcitya janako yathāprāptakriyāmasau,
asaktaḥ kartumuttasthau dinam dinapatiryathā.
bhaviṣyannānusandhatte nātītam cintayatyasau,
vartamānanimeṣaṁ tu hasannevānuvartate. Ibid., p. 81.
3. *vedānta-vijñāna suniścitārthāḥ saṁnyāsa-yogād yatayaḥ śuddhaśattvāḥ*
te brahma-lokeṣu parāntakāle parāmṛtāḥ parimucyanti sarve.

Mun. Up. II.2.6. In his commentary on this verse Śaṁkara quotes:—
śakunīnām ivākāśe jale vāricarasya ca,
padam yathā na dṛśyeta tathā jñānavatām gatiḥ. Radhakrishnan, *Bhagavadgītā*, p. 691.

saṁnyāsin who has perfected his mind enough so that it seems as an instrument of *sākṣātkāra* has a distinguished place in the *Vedānta.* An impure mind cannot intuit the Self, the renunciants are example of purity of mind. Understood accordingly, renunciation is a pure attitude of mind (*agryā buddhi*), and not an escape from life.

Jīvanmukti or Deliverance in this Life

The personal dimension of renunciation which is introvertedness (*antarmukhī*) aims at diverting the mind from the objective world (by subduing and eliminating modifications of the mind in the *manonāśa* and controlling over *vāsanās* in the *vāsanākṣaya*) to *Ātman* alone. The *Kaṭha Upaniṣad* directs us to look to our inner self with our eyes turned inwards.[1] The *Bṛhadāraṇyaka* says: "He should devote himself to the world which is only the *Ātman*; his acts never fail him, who so devotes himself."[2] The *Vedānta* holds that the realization of this *ātma-loka* constitutes freedom or deliverance. It is neither product of anything nor reducible to anything other than itself. Uncaused, unproduced, it is eternal, infinite and irrepressible. Everything else is false. The knowledge of it as Reality alone is freedom. Śaṁkara's definition of freedom is as follows : "That which is absolutely real, immutable, eternal, all penetrating like *ākāśa*, exempt from all change, ever-satisfied, impartite, self-luminous; in which neither good nor evil nor effect, nor past, nor present, nor future has any place—this incorporeal state is called freedom."[3] It is clear that freedom (*mokṣa*) for Śaṁkara is ontologically the same as *Brahma-Jñāna.*[4]

---

1. *Kaṭha Up.* II.4.1 and *Gītā* V.13.

2. *yo ha vā asmāllokāt svaṁ lokamadṛṣṭvā praiti sa anāmavidito na bhunakti. ātmānameva lokamupāsīta sa ya ātmānameva lokamupāste na hāsya karma kṣīyate. Jīvan-mukti-viveka*, p. 2.

3. *idaṁtu pāramārthikam kūṭasthanityam vyomavatsarvavyāpi sarvavikriyārahitam nityatṛptam niravayavaṁ svayamjyotisvabhāvam, yatra dharmādharmau saha kāryena kālatrayam ca nopāvartete; tadetadaśarīratvam mokṣākhyam. Śāṁkarabhāṣya*, See Bakre, *Brahmasutrabhasya*, pp. 73-74.

4. *brahmaiva hi muktyāvastyā—Ibid.*, p. 823.

Renunciation is the gradual elimination of everything other than *Brahman* and finally in the state of *Jñāna*, the elimination of the concept of *Brahman* itself. What remains absolutely unshaken is the fore-knowledge of *Brahman* and by renunciation, diversity and the multiplicity of the world, superimposed on Reality, is completely eliminated. It must never be forgotten that the overriding concern of renunciation as a philosophical attitude is the supreme Reality itself and so far as this concern is dominant, a renunciant does not lose himself in either the world or ego but finds in this world and ego an indication of transcendence which takes him beyond. Viewed from this point of view, Arapura's term of 'tranquillity' can be equally applied to the phenomenon of renunciation : "In the Indian spiritual sphere determined by the Veda, Vedānta and Buddhism" says J.G. Arapura, "whereas anxiety has always been recognized as the source of all human striving most of all in religion, Reality begins where anxiety is terminated. It has been the belief that anxiety itself is the denial of reality since it is the character of the phenomenal world of becoming, to be both contained within its bound, false as they are, and eventually burnt up along with the world. Anxiety must be totally forbidden to distort and prevent man's perception of Reality, which can mediate itself only in the mode of tranquillity."[1] He further continues: "We can speak without exaggeration or distortion what is common to Buddhism, Jainism and various systems of Hindu religion. To put it simply, it concerns a state of being, of abiding, which transcends the anxiety-laden world of becoming. And that state is tranquillity. The Upaniṣadic seers, the Vedānta teachers, the *Mahābhārata*, the *Bhagavadgītā*, the Buddha and Mahāvīra are all basically agreed on this."[2]

In order to see the real nature of this structure of renunciation, let us see the state of the *Jivanmukta*, described by other epithets such as *sthitaprajña* (one whose mind is entirely steady), *Bhagavadbhakta* (one who is devoted to God), *guṇātita* (one beyond the three properties, i.e. *sattva, rajas* and *tamas*), the *Brāhmaṇa* (one who has realized the *Brahman*), *Brahmasaṁstha* (one who is established in *Brahman*) and *Ativarṇāśramin* (one

1. Arapura, *Religion as Anxiety and Tranquillity*, p. 77.
2. *Ibid.*

beyond the four *varṇas* and four *āśramas*). Vidyāraṇya defines the state of the *Jīvanmukta* : "He is the true *Jīvanmukta*, for whom the phenomenal world, wherein he moves and acts, ceases to exist, leaving alone the all-pervading Eternal Noumenon".[1] Renunciation by those who have realized the supreme truth is called the renunciation-of-the-enlightened (*vidvat-saṁnyāsa*). This state is different from the renunciation-of-the seeker (*vividiṣā-saṁnyāsa*) which takes place only after the dissolution of the body, also known as *videha-mukti*. The *Vedānta* accepts both the ideals but lays more emphasis on the enlightenment 'here and now' in this life—the realization of Consciousness, freed from all conditionings and temporality. This is known as the stage of *vyutthāna* or reversion to common life and here one does not relinquish all activities as we have seen earlier. But since egoism has vanished, activities do not emerge from lay experience but by immediate or direct intuition of the Absolute, technically known as *vidvadanubhava*.[2] Bondage consists in those functions of mind which are characterized by feelings of pleasure and pain, concomitant with action and enjoyment but after freedom has been attained through renunciation, all functions of mind have already been neutralized by cultivation of the universal love—"who sees all beings in himself and himself in all beings—he will dislike none."[3] Or as the *Gītā* puts it "He harms not self by self."[4] The foundation of the renunciation of the enlightened, therefore, is the knowledge of truth (*bodha*) and in lack of it, even perfect *vairāgya* (renunciation) is superfluous. As long as the egoism persists, *vairāgya* is incomplete. Renunciation in its broad implication is not only the renunciation of desires but renunciation of the desires of renunciation as well. The foundation of it is *Jñāna* which transforms the life of the *Jīvanmukta* to such an extent that what is unnatural behaviour

---

1. *yathāsthitamidaṁ yasya vyavahāravato'pi ca,*
astaṁ gatam sthitam vyoma sa jīvanmukta ucyate.
—*Jīvan-mukti-viveka*, p. 16.

2. Thibaut, *The Vedānta-Sūtras*, p. 357. Also see Sastri, *Pancadasi: A Treatise on Advaita Metaphysics by Swami Vidyaranya*, pp. 98-99.

3. *yas tu sarvāni bhūtāni ātmany evānupaśyati,*
sarvabhūteṣu cātmānam tato na vijugupsate. —*Īśa Up.* 6.

4. *na hinastyātamanā'tmānaṁ, Gītā,* XIII. 28. See Sastri, *The Bhagavad-Gītā*, pp. 370-72.

for others becomes natural for him. Enlightened men differ in their behaviour from the ignorants.[1]

The best way to illustrate the life of an enlightened person is to look at the life of a saint. He is a bridge so to say between the earthly and supra-earthy, the temporal and eternal. It was pointed out that if the relation between the one and the other were that of otherness, the ideal of the *Jīvanmukti* would be an impossibility and so the deliverance. The *Vedānta* presents a scheme of spirituality (*Ādhyātmavāda*) which bases itself on a complete mingling between cosmic interest and the individual interest, between means and the end. The function of renunciation in the life of the enlightened person is to annihilate the gulf between the two which divides him from the rest of the mankind. It is to create a new attitude towards mankind. A man who is united within can only unite the world and not a man who is divided. It should be clearly noted however, that for the *Vedānta*, this transformation of the attitude of the enlightened person is not an achievement but purely a realization. It is the very nature of the Self which happens to have been forgotten. This position again strengthens the spirit of renunciation. The enlightened person is not doing any mercy to mankind and as long as he suffers with this attitude he is not enlightened. As we pointed out earlier, this is his natural way (*svabhāva*). We can hardly speak of renunciation as a means in an ordinary sense for achieving the enlightened nature. Only in this sense, we have spoken of renunciation at the acosmic level, as equivalent to *Brahma-Jñāna*. A renunciant in the *Vedānta* is one who is *Brahma-saṁstha*. It is the contention of the *Vedānta* that freedom is possible by renunciation alone. The paths advocated by other systems can at best lead to the purification of mind. Renunciation in its final meaning, therefore, is nothing but self-knowledge (*ātma-bodhi*). Śaṁkara while commenting on the *Gītā* calls the *mukta* as *Jñāna-Vijñāni* (a man of knowledge).[2] Manu describes the stages of saintliness in the following way :

---

1. *yā niśā sarvabhūtānāṁ tasyāṁ jāgarti saṁyamī*
yasyāṁ jāgrati bhūtāni sā niśā paśyato muneḥ. —*Gītā*. II. 69.
2. *Jñānavijñānatṛptātma*, *Gītā*, VI-8. See Sastry, *The Bhagavad-Gita*, p. 188.

> That action which is performed with a view to obtaining something here or hereafter is called *pravṛtti*, that action is *nivṛtti* which is done without attachment and with insight or knowledge. Following the first course of action (in accordance with *dharma*) man attains similarity to gods; pursuing disinterested activity, he transcends the five elements. He who sees the *Ātman* in all existents, and all the existents in the *Ātman*, such a person, sacrificing to the self (alone), attains identity with the self-luminous *Brahman*.[1]

The *Bhagavad-Gītā* describes this state as follows :

> O son of Pritha, when a man puts away all cravings of the mind, and is satisfied in the Self through (the joy of) self, then he is called stable of mind. The sage whose mind remains untroubled in sorrows, who is free of desires amid pleasure, and from whom passion, fear and anger have passed away, is called of stable mind. He who is without attachment to anything and meeting with good and evil, neither rejoices nor complains, his mind is said to be firmly settled. He who withdraws the senses from the objects of the senses on all sides as tortoise draws in its limbs (into the shell)—his mind has become firmly set . . . enjoying the various sense objects with the senses under control and free from attachment and aversion, the man with mastery over himself attains composure of mind . . . . He who having given up all desires without attachment and egoism, attains peace.[2]

The life of a renunciant (*akāmayamāna*) is described in the *Bṛhadāraṇyaka* : "And now of him who desires not—He who is without desire, free from desire, whose desires are stilled, whose desire is the Self, his vital breaths do not depart, but *Brahman* is he and into *Brahman* is he resolved."[3] The *Paramahaṁsopaniṣad* has described at great length the renunciation of the enlightened. The *parama-haṁsa*, it might be remarked, is one who knows the essence of truth in this world and therefore it is equivalent

1. Buhler, *The Laws of Manu*, XII. 89-91.
2. *Bhagavad-Gītā*, II.55-58, 64-65 and 69-72.
3. *iti nu kāmayamānaḥ; athākāmayamānaḥ, yo'kāmo niṣkāma āpta-kāma ātmākāmaḥ, na tasya prāṇā utkrāmanti, brahmaiva san brahmāpyeti. Bṛ. Up.*, IV. 4.6,

to the *Jivanmukta*. The state of the *paramahaṁsa* has been differentiated from the state of the *haṁsa*, who knows the essence of truth in that world (the world of gods or pitṛs). Both are the ascetics (*saṁnyāsins*) but the *paramahaṁsa* is completely enlightened and is a man of self-knowledge. "The curiosity of the *paramahaṁsa*", remarks Śrī Vidyāraṇya, "is not aroused by all this wonderous panorama, as he knows fully well that these powers of the Self-that-is-all-consciousness manifest themselves in diverse ways."[1] The *Saṁnyāsa Upaniṣad* also discusses in detail the life of the ascetic who forsakes the world for the life of *jñāna*.[2] In many works of the *Dharmaśāstras*, we find a detailed discussion on the types of renunciants. The *Mahābhārata*, for example, categorizes them in four types, namely *Kuṭīcaka*, *Bahūdaka*, *Haṁsa* and *Paramahaṁsa*, each later one being superior to each preceding one.[3] The *Kuṭīcaka* resides in a secluded hermitage. The *bahūdaka* goes from one sacred place to another. The *haṁsa* flies like a swan to the seventh heaven. The *paramahaṁsa* enjoys liberation in this very life. Śaṁkara has mostly discussed the life of the *paramahaṁsa*. The *paramahaṁsa* is again, either the seeker after knowledge (*jijñāsu*) or the enlightened (*jñānin*), also known as *vividiṣā-saṁnyāsa* (renunciation of the seeker) and *vidvat-saṁnyāsa* (renunciation of the enlightened). The *vividiṣā-saṁnyāsa* represents the cosmic ideal of renunciation which comes about by the strong desire for knowledge generated in the proper manner and includes the performance of religious duties, devotion to God, renunciation of the desire-impelled action, the performance of the duties associated with the *varṇāśrama* etc. The latter type, i.e. *vidvat-saṁnyāsa* is pure life of *jñāna* or self-knowledge and therefore it represents the acosmic ideal of renunciation which is a life of complete and absolute freedom. For the former, morality still holds good, but for the latter, it does not apply.

---

1. *cidātmanīmā ittham prasphuranti hi śaktayaḥ,*
ityasyāścāryajāleṣu nābhyudeti kutūhalam. Jīvan-mukti-viveka, p. 140.
2. T.R.C. Dikshit, *The Saṁnyāsa Upaniṣad* (Madras : The Adyar Library, 1929). A very good commentary on the *Paramahaṁsopaniṣad* is included by Vidyāraṇya in the *Jīvan-mukti-viveka*, pp. 188-222.
3. *caturvidhā bhikṣvaste kuṭīcakabahūdakau haṁsaḥ paramahaṁsaśca yo yaḥ paścāt sottamaḥ— Anuśāsanaparva*, 141-68. See Kinjawadekar, *Sriman Mahābhārata* (*Anuśāsanaparva*), pp. 280-331.

Now the question arises : why Śaṁkara, who strictly followed the *saṁnyāsa-mārga* or *jñāna-mārga*, did accept *vividiṣā-saṁnyāsa* as preliminary to the *vidvat-saṁnyāsa ?* The answer to this question has great significance for the understanding of the personal dimension of renunciation. For the *Vedānta*, there is no separation between metaphysics and ethics. It has been repeatedly said that Śaṁkara's concept of the Absolute, being the source and essence of everything, leaves and discards nothing when viewed from the point of view of Reality which is the highest value at the same time. The inclusion of the cosmic ideal of renunciation along with the acosmic takes into account the whole structure of Indian thought in an organic form. Without entering into the metaphysical differences on this issue, as they are vast, it may be pointed out here that the concept of freedom has been worked out better in those systems of thought where the divorce of metaphysics from ethics has not taken place.[1] The *vidvat-saṁnyāsa,* which is largely a metaphysical end of life gets always nourished with the ideals as set forth in the *vividiṣā-saṁnyāsa* which represents acosmic ideal.

Status of Ethics in the Life of the Jīvanmukta

One important question which arises in this connection is the status of ethics and morality at the stage of enlightenment. In the *Taittiriya Upaniṣad*, it has been said : "He (referring to a person who has realized *Brahman*) is not troubled by thoughts like these; "Have I not done the right ? Have I done the wrong?"[2] Again in the *Āpastamba dharma-sūtra*, an ascetic who has realized *Brahman* is regarded beyond all *vidhi* (injunctions) and *niṣedha* (prohibition), that he is above the ordinary rules about truthfulness or falsehood.[3] We have in the *Bṛhadāraṇyaka*: "This is the eternal greatness of the man who realizes *Brahman* that by the actions he does, he does not add to it or detract from it. Therefore one should only know the real nature of that greatness, he on knowing *Brahman* is not affected by any evil

1. See T.M.P. Mahadevan, "Can There be Ethics without Metaphysics", in *Indian Philosophical Proceedings*, (1952), p. 130.
2. *Tai. Up.*, II.9.
3. *Āpastamba dharma-sūtra,* II.9-21.

action.[1] Similarly, the *Chāndogya* says : "Just as water does not cling to the lotus leaf, so evil deed does not cling to one who knows it."[2] The *Jābālopaniṣad* describes renunciants as beyond the pairs of *dharma* and *adharma*, *satya* and *asatya* and *śauca* and *aśauca*.[3] Similarly in his commentary on the *Vedāntasūtras*, Śaṁkara thinks that obligations exist only for those who falsely imagine the Self to be connected with the body, but for those renunciants who have realized Self, no obligations exist.[4]

All these passages assert that when *mokṣa* has been attained, a stage has been reached where morality has no longer any meaning. The ethical is transcended. The common laws of morality are significant only so far as one is striving for perfection but for one who has reached it, morality becomes meaningless. The *Vedānta* lays great stress on moral virtues only so far as self-realization is still in progress. According to Paul Deussen, morality does help the *sādhaka* but it is only auxiliary to the attainment of *Jñāna*, inasmuch as the man who leads a life of holy works is not overpowered by afflictions such as passions etc. Morality, therefore, according to him, serves two purposes: (a) as outward means (*bāhya sādhana*) of knowledge (Vedic study, sacrifice, alms, penance, fasting) and (b) the closer means (tranquillity, self-restraint, renunciation, patience, concentration etc.). But he thinks that renunciation or asceticism is still higher to morality.[5]

As we have already noticed Śaṁkara attaches supreme importance to renunciation because it alone is free from predicates of egoism. Through the annihilation of it, the very notion of moral obligations vanishes. The contrast between good and evil, rights and duties is automatically transcended after the annihilation of egoism and realization of *Jñāna*. In other words, by reaching the total renunciation of personal interest, the essential duality of the moral world is transcended. Even at the initial stage of the cosmic renunciation, the morality is transcended in

1. For details see Radhakrishnan, *The Principal Upanisads*, p. 280.
2. *yathā puṣkarapalāśa āpo na śliṣyante, evam evaṁ-vidi pāpaṁ karma 'na śliṣyata iti*. *Ch. Up.*, IV.14.3.
3. *Jābāla-Upaniṣad*, 4.
4. Thibaut, *Vedānta Sūtras*, pp. 66-68.
5. Deussen, *The Systems of the Vedānta*, p. 411.

the sense that the renunciant cares only for his duties and not rights (common morality implies both). At the latter stage, i.e., devotional stage, when the seeker serves as an instrument of *Īśvara*, the awareness of duties also disappears. At the highest stage of self-realization, when every being becomes one's own self, there is nothing left for the world of morality. Here there is no duality between the subject and object as it is the stage of complete non-duality. By extending one's self to the extent of the whole of sentient creation, man reaches a point beyond the isolation from the rest of the creation. This point is really the consummation of the entire structure of morality which serves the highest type of human ideal. B.G. Tilak remarks: "That man whose pure reason (*vyavasāyātmikā buddhiḥ*) has become capable of realizing the identity that 'there is only one *ātman* in all created things. . . it is impossible that he should commit any sin or any action obstructive of release."[1] Śaṁkara also says that laws dictating what is proper and improper do not apply to persons who have gone beyond the three constituents (*nistraiguṇye pathi vicaratāṁ ko vidhiḥ ko niṣedhaḥ*). "A man" says Gītā, "who has totally lost the feeling of individuation (*ahaṁkāra*) is untouched by sin or merit". All sense of utility, personal aggrandizement and craving cease completely. This state of freedom in the deepest and widest sense of the term, is the self-expression of the spirit. It is the state of self-guarding *gnosis*, absence of discord, cessation of pain and misery and the genesis of supreme bliss. The *Jñānin* who is a *saṁnyāsin* is not at the stage of the realization of virtues which all moralities aim at. He is revealing virtues. Renunciation, therefore, included ethics in order to transcend it. This is the stage of complete freedom where all doubts vanish completely.

Authority Bearing Testimony to Jīvanmukti
(*Svarūpasiddhiprayojanam*)

It may be asked here that the state of freedom to be reached by *saṁnyāsa* and *Jñāna* is a mere ideal, very difficult to be brought about and accomplished. In other words, it may be thought that the ideal of *Jīvanmukti* (*mokṣa* in one's life time), being

1. Tilak, *Gītā Rahasya*, pp. 511-512.

difficult to realize, is merely speculative, based on faith and not philosophy. These doubts have been raised regarding *mokṣa* as well as *saṁnyāsa*. Our answer to these questions is that there is hardly any scope for thinking like this in the *Vedānta*. No doubt, the both of them, i.e. *mokṣa* and *saṁnyāsa* are the highest ideals of life, nevertheless, they have been presented with constant awareness of a positive standard with which the Advaita Vedānta was throughout occupied. What is important to note here is that these are the ideals not for the life beyond or 'life hereafter' but a progression to be reached within the span of this life. Even those systems of thought which do not believe in the ideal of the *Jīvanmukti*, clearly recognize the possibility of a stage of life, here and now, which is tranquil, serene and free of anxieties. This state of existence, alone marks, according to all, the culmination of philosophic culture. Renunciation is central to the realization of such a state of life. A necessary corollary to such a view is that these ideals have been based on a detailed course of practical discipline which must be undergone in the midst of society for each and every system. It is, however, a fact that all these disciplines to a large extent are based on the transformation of mind arising from the gross side of human nature but this again is nourished by an implicit foreknowledge of a state of mind which is pure and refined. In absence of such realization, supported by '*śruti*', any urge towards an enlightened state cannot be sustained. In other words, the *Vedānta* starts with the certainty of a pure state of Being and the necessity of accomplishing that state. Such an ideal was already very influential as we have examined in great detail. By accepting this ideal within the limits of human experience and in the necessity of being explored and realized further, the *Vedānta* refuses to be dogmatic in eschatological sense of the term. Here it might be argued that the ideal of *videhamukti*[1] (deliverance after death) which has been accepted

1. *Videhamukti* (Freedom after death) is the deliverance of the Self from *avidyā* (*avidyāstamayo mokṣaḥ*) with the implied belief to ward off future embodiment. This position of Advaita is different from those of the *Nyāya-vaiśeṣika* and *Viśiṣṭādvaita* which believe in freedom after death. For Śaṁkara, freedom is a state of fearlessness (*abhayam*) as is renunciation in the final analysis. This has also been called *sadyomukti* (immediate deliverance). By accepting these two stages, Śaṁkara attempts a synthesis between Vedic

even by Śaṁkara, refutes the present contention but in our opinion the retention of the *videhamukti* does not present any threat to the Vedāntic ideal. In contrary, the Vedānta again harmonises the tradition.

---

and upaniṣadic thought and avoids the extreme position of suggesting *mokṣa* as a dogma in an eschatological sense. Vidyāraṇya also cites several references from the *śruti* and *smṛti* to establish this contention. See *Jīvanmukti-viveka*, pp. 122-139 and Śaṁkara's *bhāṣya* on the *Kaṭha Up.* II.3.14, (*ihaivāvidyākṛtakāmakarmabandhanairvimuktiḥ*).

Chapter Five

SOCIAL DIMENSION OF RENUNCIATION

Problems and Controversies

The central problem of this chapter is whether man's realization of Ultimate Reality for which renunciation is essential, could influence or shape the social dimension of life. In other words, can personal dimension of renunciation culminating in self-knowledge cope with the complexities and ambiguities of life which it manifestly tries to transcend by realising the depth of Reality in terms of one's own self? The task here is to examine whether the doctrine of renunciation is compatible with social progress in general or antagonistic to it. Can *Vedānta* provide some guidelines for a combination of personal dimension of renunciation and a social activism based on positive this-worldly conduct ? Are there not directions in the doctrine of renunciation itself which could be profitably re-shaped and re-interpreted to serve as a positive foundation for a harmonious functioning of society ? Needless to say these questions have provoked a host of controversies which by and large are understandable as reflecting the fact that the traditional religious values based on salvation are hard to combine with this-worldliness, as ordinarily understood. Let me say at the outset that I value all these controversies as they have stimulated many scholars for re-interpretation of Indian thought and many thoughtful Indians for a re-appraisal of their own religious tradition, but to say that the Vedāntic spirit of renunciation was irrelevant to 'inner-worldly life conduct' and value orientations seems rather to represent hypothetical projections on the *Vedānta*. The world-view with reference to which the doctrine of renunciation was explained and examined in the *Vedānta* exhibits its institutional setting in which it was most generally conceived and acted out. My contention as expressed throughout the previous sections is that the problem of renunciation emerges from the understanding of the transcendent that the phenomena reveal particularly as they are related to the former for issuing of any meanings whatsoever and are abstractions apart from their ground, viz., *Brahman*. The seeker of truth cannot find a path that issues upon salvational experience apart from this world, not by exhausting himself in it but by discovering meaning in it, the realization of which is itself freedom. The aid of such a philosophical conviction is sought in order to understand the ideal sphere of existence not by abnegating the world, society or human relationship but by harmoniously establishing them in the structure of Reality. It is possible to make a plausible case on the basis of this Vedāntic metaphysics that it generates a sense of sacred sanction for the discharge of one's obligations and responsibilities in all spheres of life, provided they are not antagonistic to the ultimate spiritual fulfilment.

What is important in this context to note is that the entire structure of the world and society, if understood in the right perspective, is a device to help the seeker towards the spiritual experience. It is by no means intelligible why this religious belief and philosophical attitude should be taken to be opposed to the ethics of everyday life and activities. Hans Mol's observation on commitment as one of the mechanisms of the sacralization process, gives support to the above contention. He observes:

> A specific identity or definition of reality or any of the other mechanisms of sacralization remain relevant in modern societies as well. All this has important implications for motivations. What one does or what one thinks one ought to do depends on the way one interprets situations. The system of meaning in which one moves has a built-in, hierarchical arrangement of priorities. The choices one makes amongst many alternatives are decisively influenced by one's assumptions about and commitments to, one's own, one's group's or one's society's identity. . . Weber paid little attention to commitment as the critical factor in the explanation of motivation. . . . The basic antithesis between rationalism and commitment, however, remains peripheral in Weber's work.[1]

1. Hans Mol, *Sacralization of Identity*, Manuscript (McMaster University, Hamilton 1974), pp. 278-279.

In the light of the above observation, let us examine the relationship between Reality, renunciation and commitment in order to see more clearly whether these factors as viewed by *Vedānta* can strengthen and sacralize systems of meaning to which it was committed. It will also be interesting to see whether renunciation is contrary to the ideal of commitment within the structure of the Vedāntic concept of Reality. Without prejudging the issue, we will also examine whether undercommitment or uncommitment has been central to some other doctrines of renunciation operating under different metaphysical structures.

Reality, Renunciation and Commitment

The main point in regard to *Brahman* as the Reality according to *Vedānta* is to determine whether its realization through renunciation is opposite to the spirit of commitment or helpful to it. I want to show here that the Vedāntic philosophy of renunciation is not a major obstacle to the ideal of commitment but that in fact it is helpful to it.[1] It is capable of providing the spiritual incentives and disciplines necessary for the growth of society without losing sight of the traditional values. Possibly we can consider some of the dominant views on the question of duties and right behaviour which manifest the principle of commitment but are still renunciatory in their implications. W. Norman Brown observes:

> Particular application of the idea of duty appears as early as in the *Rig* Veda. There it starts with the notion that our

1. For an opposite view, it is hardly necessary to suggest three main scholars' works, namely, Max Weber, *The Religion of India : The Sociology of Hinduism and Buddhism* , trans. and eds., H.H. Gerth and D. Martindale (III: Glencoe, 1958) and much controversial book, *The Protestant Ethic and the spirit of Capitalism,* trans. Talcott Parsons (New York, 1958); Sweitzer, *Indian Thought and its Development.* and David McClelland, *The Achieving Society* (New Jersey : Princeton, 1961). Max Weber's following remark is worth noting : "it could not have occurred to a Hindu to see the economic success he had attained in his calling as a sign of his salvation." *The Religion of India,* p. 326. David McClelland remarks : "Hinduism explicitly teaches that concern with earthly achievement is a snare and delusion." *The Achieving Society,* p. 357.

cosmos contains two opposing forces: that of ordered operation, progress, and harmonious cooperation of the parts; and that of disorder, chaos, destruction. The universe in which we live is held to operate under a code or set of principles to keep it going, and this code, this body of cosmic truth or order, has the name *satya* or *ṛta*. But disorder, anti-order, known as antra, is ever beating at our universe, tending to disrupt or destroy it. To keep our universe operating smoothly, every being in it has a function. . . . If he fails in performing it, to that extent the operation of the universe is impaired. The word for this individual function is *vrata* (*Rv.* 9. 112), and so important is the concept that in the post-Vedic times the word comes to mean a solemn, religious vow, to be undertaken with great seriousness and observed with unflagging zeal.[1]

The correspondence between the individual and cosmic order in the service of the social order (*ṛta*) in the *Ṛg Veda* is accomplished through rituals and sacrifices. What follows from this axiom is an identification between the social order and the order of the ritual. The main purpose of the rituals and sacrifices is explicitly to enhance and promote the cosmic order. The domestic sacrifice, for example, addressed to *Varuṇa* (the chief god of the social order) is meant for the protection of the social order. The ideal comprehends the preservation of the race and the conservation of the culture. "Sacrifice is a form of commitment" says Hans Mol, "which reinforces a system of meaning or identity by clarifying priorities. On the social or group level sacrifice upstages those beliefs and values (expressed, for instance, in favouring or reconciling gods) which strengthen the society or group. . . . Yet sacrifice also involves an act of abnegation and submission by the sacrificer (p. 100). Hubert and Mauss suggest that personal renunciation nourishes social forces and redresses equilibria that have been upset."[2]

It might be pointed out, however, that the Vedic religion also manifested some opposition between the social order and

1. W. Norman Brown, *Man in the Universe* (Berkeley and Los Angeles : University of California Press, 1966) pp. 10-11.
2. Hans Mol, *Manuscript*, pp. 291-292.

individual salvation to which we have referred at several places but these oppositions have never resulted in the denial of the cosmic order through renunciation. Since the Reality is at the back of cosmic order which is a continuous eternal process, it is the aim of religion to harness this process in the service of the cosmic order which is instrumental to the individual freedom. Stephen A. Tylor remarks: "The orthodox Sanskritic tradition has always sought to harness it to the social order, and all unorthodox traditions have originally attempted to make it serve as a means to individual freedom, to use it as a means to escape from the mutable to the immutable."[1] In the Vedāntic tradition, let us add, this escape is not as radical as in the unorthodox traditions. It is, however, a fact that the individual is not a datum of society but from the point of view of the cosmic order and cosmic ideal, he is not totally free from society. The individual, in other words, fulfils two roles and both these roles are complementary to each other: As a part of the cosmic order, he is instrumental to it and as being essentially *Brahman*, he is free from it. These two trends of thought seem to be mutually exclusive but I want to suggest here that the doctrine of renunciation which attempts a reconciliation between the two aspects, enriches itself by participating in the cosmic order without being overthrown by it. Put philosophically, *Jñāna*, radically expressed in *saṁnyāsa*, resolves the duality between the two as said in the *Mahāvākyas*. The Vedāntic ideal of renunciation does not overthrow the realm of values and commitment. In its effort to examine the cosmic ideal as put forward by the Vedas, it does not repudiate the Vedas but accommodates them. It may be granted here that this accommodation may not be very explicit in the *Upaniṣads* but it is difficult to deny its overwhelming importance in the Advaita Vedānta. As we have pointed out in the typology of renunciation, that this adjustment was found necessary due to the direct threat to the positive ideal of renunciation as posed by some uncompromisingly ascetic trends of thought. This transformation brought out far-reaching changes in the structure of Indian society. In

1. Stephen A. Tylor, *India : An Anthropological Perspective* (California : Goodyear Publishing Company, Inc., 1973), p. 23.

the recent years, we find a re-thinking of Vedāntic ideal on this pattern of thought on the basis of which some of the strictures against the spirit of the Indian thought in general and the Advaita Vedānta in particular can be challenged. What I want to suggest here is that the cosmic ideal of the Advaita Vedānta (representing the cosmic order linked with *dharma*) and the acosmic ideal (representing *mokṣa* and *saṁnyāsa*) are not contradictory life-orientations but complementary to each other. To be in the world is to be bound to the cosmic order, its obligations and commitment and to be *Brahman* is again to participate in *Brahman* as a free individual. Many Indian scholars on India show the same spirit in these matters which are not foreign to the Vedāntic ideals.[1] Milton Singer's following remark is very relevant to our point under consideration:

> On prima facie grounds, one could make a pretty plausible case for the thesis that Hindu metaphysics could produce just those kinds of "character" and "character traits" which Weber regarded as necessary for a modern industrial society; a belief in an orderly universe subject to deterministic laws; the ability to anticipate a course of events and to behave accordingly, with the possibility of control based on knowledge; a strong sense of responsibility for one's actions and their consequences, and a capacity to organize one's life under a systematic methodical discipline which will maximize the goals one has set oneself. It is also plausible to argue, as I have elsewhere, that these secular character traits are given a religious and transcendental sanction, not unlike that of a Protestant ethic, in the *Bhagavad Gītā* and in other Hindu scriptures. And there is evidence, as I have suggested for the actual existence of devout Hindus who manifest these traits in different roles and occupations—business, industry, farming, government, education, religion and elsewhere.[2]

1. Examples, Rabindra Nath Tagore, *The Religion of Man* (London : Allen and Unwin, 1931) ; S. Radhakrishnan, *The Hindu View of Life* (London : Allen and Unwin, 1927) and V. Raghavan, "Some Leading Ideas of Hindu Thought", *The Vedānta Kesari* (Madras, Feb., 1955).
2. Singer, "Religion and Social Change in India: A Max Weber Thesis, phase three", *Economic Development and Cultural Change*, p. 501. Also see Milton

Perhaps I should balance my discussion of the above possibilities in the *Vedānta* by highlighting the spirit of renunciation as a sanctifying principle in every sphere of life. As I pointed out earlier, morality or religion in itself is of no interest to the *Vedānta.* It must be developed and fulfilled only with reference to the metaphysical orientations of life. In other words, business, economics, farming or industry, morality and religion, pursued by individuals for their own benefits, cannot have the metaphysical sanction but at the same time they cannot be denied of their legitimate status on pragmatic grounds. The *Vedānta* does not lose sight of the differences between the pragmatic truth and the metaphysical validity of that pragmatic truth. The pragmatic truth must be brought forward in order to serve the collectivity in a spirit of renunciation. A direction towards the fulfilment of this ideal is again made metaphysically valid by denying the 'objective' status of the collectivity and bringing it at par with oneself. Whether this spiritual recipe for the pragmatic truth is likely to materialize or not, is another matter. What I am saying here is that the Vedāntic concept of Reality, instead of being taken as an obstacle in the ideal of commitment, may be taken as a further extension of the notion of commitment, which in turn disapproves of egoism, narrow-mindedness, greed, acquisitiveness, domination and exploitation. The *Vedānta*, in other words, is not by any means, inconsistent with values and behaviour or dynamic social activism, provided they are carried out in inwardly detached spirit and with disinterested motives. The detached spirit (renunciation) is a way of purifying the commitment without undermining it in any way.

One point must be clarified here. From what we have stated so far, regarding the disinterested motive or detached spirit, it should not be taken that the *Vedānta* recommends a life without purpose. It should rather mean here a life of 'disinterested interest' only so far as it turns our mind from appropriating the results of our actions, rather than actions themselves. This attitude does not minimize the importance of responsibility which I think remains at its maximum. What remains at the back of

---

Singer, "The Great Tradition in a Metropolitan City: Madras", *Traditional India : Structure and Change.* (Philadelphia: American Folklore Society, 1959).

obligation and responsibility, according to the Vedāntic ideal of renunciation, is not only disregard of the fruits and consequences of the action, but also conception of being *kartā* (doer) and *bhoktā* (enjoyer). In this wider sense, it takes as its essential basis the pure activities (*śuddha karmāṇi*) which are natural to man and no view of life can disregard them. The course of natural activity is endangered only when it lacks the ideal of renunciation and is utilized for selfish ends. Renunciation, therefore, eliminates anxieties, doubts and despondency, which dominate over natural activity. The way to do it is not by resort ing to the life of loneliness but realizing the nature of oneself which is the central theme of the *Vedānta*. Only in this sense, we have described renunciation as an enlightened attitude.

Institutionalization of Renunciation

The role assigned to the phenomenon of renunciation from the point of view of the commitment to discharge one's obligations without the idea of recompense, acquires enormous social vitality when viewed from the institutional perspective. The treatment of renunciation remains incomplete without taking this dimension into account. Renunciation as an individual practice gets modified when it is institutionalized and functions as an aspect of social organization in general. This is a very important religious phenomenon for understanding the social dimension of renunciation. It refutes, on the one hand, that it is a complete withdrawal, which cannot obviously be an institution, and on the other, which is equally important, it refutes the theory that renunciation cannot be applied to the people universally. Taken in a broad sense, renunciation as an institution here means the life of the people, united for a specific purpose, which as the religion of the entire society, takes place as a kind of sociological corrective. This aspect of renunciation is very crucial, especially for a tradition like *Vedānta* which does not have any founder as such. The renunciants, therefore, serve the purpose of preserving and transmitting the *sanātanadharma*, as being renowned for their self-control and spiritual discipline, and perpetuating a spirit of renunciation in the society which is traditionally committed to such an ideal. In order to examine these questions in more details, let us turn to the philosophy of renunciation as practised in the Hindu society in general and the *Maṭha* (religious centre) in particular. Let me say at the outset that Paul Deussen's interpretation of renunciation as an institution as recognized in the teaching of the *Upaniṣads* has been strictly followed by me.[1] In a sense, as I discussed earlier, this institutional aspect was implicitly recognized in the Vedas. The Vedāntic explanation of the *Maṭha* is entirely on the Vedic and Upaniṣadic lines and not on the Buddhist lines as suggested by Sukumar Dutt.[2] The reasons for this contention will be further examined later.

Renunciation as the Basis of the Hindu Society : A Study of the Four Āśramas

The word '*āśrama*' is derived from the Sanskrit root '*śrama*' and therefore it means 'to exert oneself'. The *āśramas* are four in number, namely (1) the *brahmacarya* (student life), (2) the *gṛhastha* (the householder's life), (3) the *vānaprastha* (the retired life) and (4) the *saṁnyāsa* (life of complete renunciation). Without going into the controversy whether in the beginning (Vedic and Upaniṣadic times) there were only three *āśramas* or four *āśramas*[3] which has been briefly discussed before, I would like to examine here the importance of the *saṁnyāsa* as an institution in the Indian tradition and particularly in the *Vedānta* and the widespread controversy over the transition from one stage to the other. It will also be interesting to see and examine the extent to which renunciation conditions each and every *āśrama*.

Pointing out the relevance of an ascetic life for social solidarity, E. Durkheim says :

> It is even a good thing that the ascetic ideal be incarnated eminently in certain persons whose speciality, so to speak, it is to represent, almost with excess, this aspect of the ritual

1. Deussen, *The Philosophy of the Upanisads*, pp. 411-412.
2. Dutt, *Buddhist Monks and Monasteries of India*, pp. 45-47.
3. P. M. Modi, "Development of the System of Āśramas", *Proceedings and Translation of the Seventh All Indian Oriental Conference* (Baroda, 1935), pp. 316-17.

life, for they are like so many living models, inciting to effort. Such is the historic role of great ascetics. When their deeds and acts are analysed in detail, one asks himself what end they have. He is struck by the fact that there is something excessive in the disdain they profess for all that ordinarily impassions men. But these exaggerations are necessary to sustain among the believers as sufficient disgust for an easy life and common pleasures. It is necessary that an elite put the end too high, if the crowd is not to put it too low. It is necessary that some exaggerate, if the average is to remain at a fitting level.[1]

The kind of disdain and disgust, Durkheim is linking with asceticism, might be reduced to its minimal when asceticism emerges from the real conviction of the realization of higher self fulfilment. In other words, a society in which renunciation is prescribed as a duty for the sake of greater self-realization, asceticism or renunciation becomes a part of life and need not be generated from a disgust or disdain of the worldly life. This might be also due to the fundamental recognition of the Vedānta that there is no clear-cut distinction between the secular and the sacred. By bridging the gulf between the two world-views, renunciation takes place as a matter of course and transforms the secular into the sacred and vice versa. Renunciation emerging from despair, disgust or doubt, as the *Gītā* puts it, is attachment(*rāga*), not detachment (*vairāgya*) and shows the weakness of heart (*hṛdayadaurbalyaṁ*).[2] Renunciation generating from disgust has been regarded by Vidyāraṇya as of a dull type.[3]

Renunciation is a real force of life and is a well-known phenomenon of Indian life even today. Milton Singer's following remark shows the significance of the point :

---

1. Emile Durkheim, *Elementary Forms of Religious Life* (New York : Collier Books, 1961), p. 355.

2. *Klaibyaṁ mā sma gamaḥ pārtha nai 'tat tvayy' upapadyate, kṣudraṁ hṛdaya-daurbalyaṁ tyaktvottiṣṭha paraṁtapa.—Gītā* II. 3.

3. *putradāradhanādīnāṁ nāśe tātkālikī matiḥ, dhik saṁsāramitidṛkṣyādvirakter-mandatā hi sā.—Jīvan-mukti-viveka*, p. 1.

The theme of the king or rich man who gives up everything for the sake of a spiritual principle is very common in Indian literature. The characterisation of this theme in the stories of Rāma, the Pāṇḍavas, Hariścandra, are almost universally known and beloved by Indians everywhere. And it is not only the mighty and rich who are expected to renounce, for in the traditional Indian theory of the stages of life, the householder who has discharged his responsibilities to his family should renounce his possessions and eventually all family ties to become a sannyāsi or holy man who lives on alms."[1]

Without denying the importance of this phenomenon in the Indian tradition, questions may still be asked pertaining to its relevance to the economic growth in India. Most of the scholars have held the traditional value system of India (includiug that of renunciation) responsible for the lack of economic growth.[2]

F.M. Cornford correctly points out that most of the controversies which arise in the philosophical discussions are largely based on ordinary assumptions which philosophers do not care to expound as they are taken for granted or are obvious.[3] When

1. Singer, "Cultural Values in India's Economic Development' : p. 83.

2. See, for example, Kusum Nair, *Blossoms in the Dust* (New York : Frederick A. Praeger, 1962), pp. 192-193; Vera Anstey, *The Economic Development of India* (third ed.; London : Longman Green and Company, 1936), p. 17; Abe Dubois, *Hindu Manners, Customs and Ceremonies*, ed., Henry K. Beauchamp (third ed.; Oxford : The Clarendon Press, 1906), pp. 96-97 and Charles Trevelyan, *On the Education of the People of India* (London: 1838), pp. 83-84. (All the above scholars are of the opinion that the religious tenets and practices of Hinduism have stood as greatest obstacles in the economic advancement of India.) For a general survey of this problem, see V. Mishra, *Hinduism and Economic Growth* (Bombay: Oxford University Press, 1962).

3. "If we look beneath the surface of philosophic discussion, we find that its course is largely governed by assumptions that are seldom or never mentioned.. .because it is taken for granted as obvious.. .when we try to recover the outlook so framed and limited, we shall distort the picture if we unconsciously substitute our own perspectives for theirs." F. M. Cornford, *The Laws of Motion in Ancient Thought* (Cambridge: Cambridge University Press, 1931), p. 12.

we think of such matters as economic growth of society, it is useless on the part of the philosophers to expound its necessity as it is left for sensitive readers to deduce it from the world-views of those philosophers. Most of the critics of the Vedāntic theory of *saṁnyāsa* have failed to link the economic growth with the *āśrama* theory, culminating in *saṁnyāsa* as the highest ideal of life. Albert Schweitzer's well known remark needs hardly any introduction. He thinks that the *āśrama* theory inconsistently relates 'affirmation' of life with the 'negation' through *saṁnyāsa*[1] and equates it with a 'do-nothing' kind of attitude of the renunciates. Schweitzer wrongly takes the word 'renunciation' in a very limited and distorted sense and thinks it is against everything which is 'positive', in the way he understands it. I would like to show here very briefly that even the *saṁnyāsa* can provide great incentives for such activities like economic development and progress of the society in its own way.

The life of *saṁnyāsa*, it is needless to deny, helps a smooth transfer of the property within the family and provides an incentive for the hard work to the next generation. The property, thus acquired, serves a better purpose than a property acquired for self-aggrandizement. This tendency of life, when combined with other incentives can result in a voluntary redistribution of the wealth without any grievance or bitterness. The *sampattidāna* (donation of the property), introduced by Vinoba Bhave is based on the ideal of renunciation—"There is one thing which we will demonstrate through *sampattidāna* : that non-possession is a source for social good. We have long known that non-possession brings about individual purification. We have to realize that it can also serve as powerful means of social well-being. We have to prove that it is not only spiritually efficacious but it can help us in constructing better and richer worldly life . . . . The people of India would understand this idea more speedily than others. It is not difficult for people here to perceive that we as people are all one. The reason is our seers have taught the ideal to us from very ancient times till today."[2]

1. Schweitzer, *Indian Thought and its Development*, pp. 39-40.
2. Vinoba Bhave, "The Kingdom of Benevolence through Dana", in K. Satchidananda Murty, ed. *Readings in Indian History, Philosophy and Politics* (London : George Allen and Unwin Ltd., 1967) pp. 189-194'.

Elucidating the same ideal further, he points out: "I do not beg it. I would have begged, had I been asking for myself.... They still ask me why I am going about begging for alms. They do not know that the great Śaṁkarācārya has defined *dāna* as *dānaṁ samvibhāgaḥ*, i.e., equitable distribution....Finally in their service, they should give up all and voluntarily sacrifice everything."[1] The ancient authorities Bhave is referring to are the authorities of the Veda, *Upaniṣad*, Buddhism, and Śaṁkara. The *Ṛg Veda* affirms that 'He that eats by himself will keep his sin to himself.[2] The broader implication of this principle has been worked out in the life of the *Maṭha*, whose property belongs to the *Maṭha* as collectivity. The *Vedānta* insofar as it does away with all sense of belongingness to the individual would lend support to an effort to dissolve private property. In this sense, it is easy to see that the Vedāntic concept of renunciation, being rooted in the highest truth, is not irrelevant to the deliverance of mankind from economic problems which belong to the realm of the 'lower truth' (*vyāvahārika satya*). The ethic of economic activity, in other words, is somehow to be united with the ideal of self-abnegation at the individual and cosmic levels. The ideal of Vinoba Bhave was obviously, Mahatma Gandhi, who is not known only for his asceticism but also his inner-worldly asceticism.

Renunciation of the fruits (results), for Gandhi, does not imply indifference either towards action or the proper understanding of the result of action: "In regard to every action one must know the result that is expected to follow, the means thereto and the capacity for it. He who is being thus equipped, is without desire for the result, and is yet wholly engrossed in the due fulfilment of the task before him, is said to have renounced the fruits of actions."[3] Gandhi applies this interpretation of the *Gītā* to economic life:

> The common belief is that the religion is always opposed to material good. One cannot act religiously in mercantile and

1. *Ibid.*, p. 190.
2. '*Kevalāgho bhavati kevalādī*', *Ṛg Veda* 117.6. Also *agham sa kevalaṁ bhuṅkte yaḥ pacatyātmakāraṇāt. Yajñaśiṣṭānnam hyetat satāmannam vidhīyate.*—*Manusmṛti*, III. 118.
3. Desai, *The Gospel of Selfless Action or the Gītā according to Gandhi* p. 131.

> such other matters. There is no place for religion in such pursuits; religion is only for attainment of salvation. . . .In my opinion the author of the *Gītā* has dispelled this delusion. . . . Thus according to the *Gītā*, all acts that are incapable of being performed without attachment are taboo. This golden rule saves mankind from many pitfalls. . . murder, lying, dissoluteness and the like must be regarded as sinful and therefore taboo. Man's life thus becomes simple and from that simpleness springs peace.[1]

Gandhi gives a different turn to the ideal of sacrifice (*yajña*) which means an act of service (body-labour in service of others). Sacrifice is also the service of the gods and this can only be accomplished by sharing everything with others. He who does not do it is verily a thief.[2] But this ideal of sharing everything with others, according to Gandhi rests on disciplined behaviour which is essential for the modern society:

> Man must reduce his daily conduct to mechanical regularity and precision, but he must do so intelligently. . .one has but to withdraw the Self, withdraw attachment to fruit from all action, and then not only mechanical precision but security from all wear and tear will be ensured.[3]

It can be easily seen here that the theory of body-labour (*kāya-karma*) becomes a *yajña* (sacrifice), when performed selflessly for others. What Gandhi is trying to suggest here is that the philosophy of renunciation is not an obstacle in the economic development of the society but it is capable of generating a 'this-worldly asceticism' without dissociating itself from the Vedāntic metaphysical structure.

In the light of the above discussion, such belief as "it could not have occurred to a Hindu to prize the rational transformation of the world in accordance with matter-of-fact considera-

---

1. Ibid., p. 132.
2. *Iṣṭān bhogān hi vo devā dāsyante yajñabhāvitāḥ, tair dattān apradāyaibhyo yo bhuṅkte stena eva saḥ.* —*Gītā*, III.12.
3. Desai, *The Gospel of Selfless Action or the Gītā According to Gandhi*, pp. 182-183.

tions and to undertake such transformation as an act of obedience to a divine will,"[1] seems to be unjustified. The Rudolphs observe here: "The disposition to work, save and rationally allocate time and resources in order to realize given goals is not necessarily modern. It appears, for example, among religious orders, both East, and West, where self-control and asceticism in the service of spiritual ends find expression."[2] The fundamental difference between the classical and modern approaches to the understanding of these issues lies in the fact that for the classicists it was the essence of religion that determined other considerations whereas for the moderns, other considerations in terms of functions and consequences, determine the essence of religion. For the *Vedānta* and neo-Vedāntins in India, essence and consequences are inseparable but it is the essence that bestows and everything else just receives. Religion is the phenomenon not reducible to faulty rationality of individual emotional trauma.

The philosophical basis of renunciation is the spirit of human unity which requires as its pre-requisite the discharge of one's obligations as a man towards all living beings. Gandhi says:

> To be true to such religion, one has to lose oneself in continuous and continuing service of all life. Realization of truth is impossible without a complete merging of oneself in, and in identification with, this limitless ocean of life. Hence, for me, there is no escape from social service, there is no happiness on earth beyond and apart from it. Social service here must be taken to include every department of life. In this scheme, there is nothing low and nothing high. For all is one, though we seem to be many.[3]

Such an approach can only remove the isolationism and escapism. To call the doctrine of renunciation a philosophy of isolationism or escapism is a strange ironical fact.

1. Max Weber, *The Religion of India*, p. 326.
2. Rudolphs, *The Modernity of Tradition*, pp. 219-220.
3. S. Radhakrishnan and J.H. Muirhead, eds., *Contemporary Indian Philosophy* (London : George Allen and Unwin Ltd., 1936), p. 18.

Śaṁkara and the Founding of the Maṭhas

Now we shall return to the problem of another phenomenon of institutionalization of renunciation in the form of several religious centres known as the *Maṭhas*, as well as the religious communities known as the *Pariṣads*. The following discussion treats institutionalization precisely from the Advaitic perspective of renunciation without taking into account the various types of it in the Indian religious tradition. It is unfortunate that no work, as far as we know, has been done in this general area. The necessity of the institutionalization of renunciation in the *Vedānta* emerged from the conviction of its promulgation to others as an unbroken Indian religious tradition. The reinforcement of such an ideal is a continuing one and is grounded on the conviction that the basis of it is real and can not only strengthen the spiritual experience of the committed individuals but also foster the unity of society on the foundation of the ideal of renunciation. Renunciation, therefore, becomes a mode of community life, or more broadly speaking, a community act. According to tradition, Śaṁkara founded these religious centres for the purpose of revitalizing Vedic thought. If this were true—that is if tradition is right—it would be highly significant. Śaṁkara is said to have divided India into four zones in order to cover the whole country and established a *maṭha* in each one, viz., *Jyoti* at Badri in the North, *Śāradāpīṭha* at Dvāravatī in the West, *Govardhana* at Purī in the East and *Śṛṅgerī* in the South. He also organized the *saṁnyāsins* into ten orders, known as *Daśanāmis*, namely, (1) *Giri* (hill), (2) *Puri*, (city), (3) *Bhārati* (learning), (4) *Vana* (wood), (5) *Āraṇya* (forest), (6) *Parvata* (mountain), (7) *Sāgara* (ocean), (8) *Tīrtha* (temple), (9) *Āśrama* (hermitage) and (10) *Sarasvatī* (true knowledge), forming the suffixes to the names taken by monks of these orders.[1]

1. *Triveṇī-saṅgame tīrthe tat-tvam-asyādilkṣaṇe, snāyāt tattvārthabhāvena tīrtha-nāmā sa ucyate. āśrama-grahaṇe prauḍhaḥ āśāpāśavivarjitaḥ yātāyātavinirmuktaḥ etad āśramalakṣaṇam. suramye nirjane deśe vāsaṁ nityam karoṭi yaḥ, āśāpāśavinirmuktaḥ vana-nāmā sa ucyate., āraṇye saṁsthito nityam ānandam nandane vane tyaktvā sarvam idam viśvam āraṇyam laksaṇam kila. vāso girivare nityam Gītā-bhāṣye hi tatparaḥ, gambhīrācalabuddhiśca girināmā sa ucyate. vaset parvatamūleṣu prauḍho yo dhyāna-tatparaḥ, sārāsaraṁ vijānāti parvataḥ parikīrtitaḥ. vaset sāgaragambhīre dhanaratna-*

All these names of the ascetics are very significant and stand for such positive virtues as serenity, communion with *parabrahman* (Godhead), learning, steadfast knowledge as stable as a mountain, truth as wide and deep as the ocean, etc. It seems that they were *saṁnyāsins* in the sense of the *Brahma-saṁstha* (established in *Brahman*).

Śaṁkara is said to have consolidated and organized these *Maṭhas* bringing them under regular discipline, still known as *mahānuśāsana* (great discipline.) "The plaintiff of the *maṭha*", he is quoted to have said, "should be pure, expert in Vedic lore and proficient in *yoga* and all *śāstras* and should have his senses controlled. Such a man should sit as the head of a *maṭha* as my representative. Otherwise, if anyone becomes seated, he should be dislodged."[1] The duties of these heads inclu e their travelling around for preaching to the people, keeping in direct touch with the people, counselling and maintaining the order of the *varṇāśramadharma*.[2] All the riches of the *maṭha* should be invested for the propagation of the *dharma*. The head of the *maṭha* must be indifferent to the property of the *maṭha* like the lotus-leaf and fix his mind on *Brahman*.[3] The heads might be permitted to live in the style of a king or god.[4]

It is our contention here that these *maṭhas* serve a very important function as an agency of hope, courage and strength to the

---

parigrahaḥ, maryādaścānullaṅghyeta sāgaraḥ parikīrtitaḥ. sarvajñānavaśo nityaṁ sarvavādī kavīśvaraḥ, saṁsāra-sāgare sārābhijño yo sa sarasvatī. vidyābhāreṇa sampūrṇaḥ sarvabhāraṁ parityajet, duḥkhabhāram na jānāti Bhāratī parikīrt taḥ. Jñāna-tattvena sampūrṇaḥ pūrṇatattve pade sthitaḥ parabrahmarato nityam purīnāmā sa ucyate.

Maṭhāmnāya, quoted by Chakraborty, *Asceticism in Ancient India*, pp.179-80.

1. *śucirjitendriyo vedavedāṅgādiviśāradaḥ yogajñah sarvaśāstrāṇām sa madāsthānam āpnuyāt uktalakṣaṇasampannaḥ syāccen maṭhapīṭhabhāg bhavet, anyathā rūḍhapīṭho'pi nigrahārho manīṣiṇām.*

   Ibid., p. 185.

2. *svasvarāṣṭrapratiṣṭhityai saṁcāraḥ suvidhīyatām, maṭhe tu niyataṃ vāsaḥ-ācāryasya na yujyate. varṇāśramasadācāra asamābhirye prasādhitaḥ, rakṣaṇīyāstu evaite sve sve bhāge yathāvidhiḥ.*

   Ibid.

3. *Kevalaṁ dharmam uddiśya vibhavo brahmacetasām, vihitaścopakārāya padmapatranayam vrajet.*

   Ibid.

4. *deva-rājopacārāṁśca yathāvadanupālayet.*

   Ibid.

people in face of difficulties. These centres were created to provide an example and inspiration to the society by those ascetics who "exemplify in an exaggerated form the inhibition of natural drives, and such inhibition is a prerequisite for the conduct of all social life."[1] There is a continual and vital relationship between the *maṭha* and the society which calls for the members of the *maṭha* to be active in society. This fact is of great significance in assessing their relation to society. They do not lack the community basis and in fact it is difficult to notice their complete separateness from the society and their values and also their involvement in them in a disinterested manner.[2] This ideal seems to be based on the concept of the *avatāra* (incarnation) which the Vedāntins value very highly. It could be argued that one of the consequences of this religious situation is that the door remains wide open for the *saṁnyāsins* to legitimate and sanction even some of the socio-political activities which might otherwise remain outside their spiritual realm. In the history of the Indian religious thought such occurrences are not rare. B.M. Barua's following ramarks are worthy of noting :

> ...it shows that although with the wanderers in general the subject of constant and habitual discussion comprised all social and political questions ana though the discussion of philosophical problems was but a hobby, so to speak, they were not altogether indifferent to the great spiritual striving which was going on in the country all round, side by side with its intellectual and material progress.[3]

The present formulation is quite in consonance with the general belief of the *Vedānta* that Reality cannot be worked out in rigid isolation from other values and institutions. Since the *maṭhas* are the centres for the cultivation of the ultimate value which can also legitimate other values and institutions, their

1. G. Obeyesekere, "The Great Tradition and the Little in the Perspective of Sinhalese Buddhism", *Journal of Asian Studies*, Vol. 22 (2), 1963.

2. It may be noted here that the *saṁnyāsins* of these *maṭhas* are not required like the Bauddha *bhikkhus* or Jain *sādhus* to remain at one place during the four months of the rainy season. If they go on their wanderings, they are generally expected not to stay at one place for more than three days.

3. Barua, *A History of Pre-Buddhistic Indian Philosophy*, p. 349.

isolation from the established authorities and power structures can hardly be justified. It is very curious to note that in the Indian religious setting the relationship between the religious authority and other social structures has never ended in failure. In fact, this close relationship between the ultimate sanction of religion as exemplified in the lives of the *saṁnyāsins* and functionally necessary values of the society have continued to exercise a great influence on the Hindu life even today. The present analysis provides an element of corrective to a wide spread belief on the part of some of the scholars who hold that the other-worldly interpretation is antagonistic to an activist and this-worldly one. Whether this or another interpretation is valid depends on the appreciation of the meanings with which they are infused and purposes to which they are relevant. In fact, those meanings can equally be harnessed for the purpose of resolving the modern predicaments.

Another very important function served by those *maṭhas* is the work of *sanskritization* of the culture.[1] According to M.N. Srinivas, "*Sanskritization* is the process by which a "low" Hindu caste, or trible or other group, changes its customs, rituals, ideology, and way of life in the direction of a high caste, and frequently, "twice-born" caste."[2] It should be carefully noted here that the life of *maṭhas* as established by Śaṁkara does not suffer from any of this kind of limitation. A *saṁnyāsin* is above the caste system and also above the rituals and customs: "... from the knowledge of oneness of the supreme *ātman* and his own self, all sense of distinction between the two, stands destroyed;—that is the daily austerity."[3] In the life of the *maṭha*, where *Jñāna* is regarded supreme, there is no distinction between one caste and the other at that stage. In the light of this observation, it can be said that the *maṭhas* provide an opportunity for such

1. I have borrowed this word from M. N. Srinivas, *Social Change in Modern India* (Berkeley and Los Angeles : University of California Press, 1969), p. 1.

2. *Ibid.*, p. 6.

3. *Jīvan-mukti-viveka*, p. 207. *idam brahma, idam kṣatram, ime lokāḥ, ime devāḥ, imāni bhūtāni, idam sarvaṁ yad ayam ātmā. Bṛ. Up.* II. 4.6. The *Upadeśasāhasrī* describes the same ideal. Cf. Jagadanand, *The Upadeśasāhasri of Sri Śaṅkarācārya*, pp. 80-89.

sanskritization. When Śaṁkara in his commentary on *Bṛhadāraṇyaka Upaniṣad* says that only the *Brāhmaṇa* can be entitled to the state of *saṁnyāsin*, he is not speaking in terms of the caste system but in terms of one who is a *brahmasaṁstha* (established in *Brahman*). He presupposes the acquisition of *Jñāna* on the part of the *Brāhmaṇas*. In this sense, it might equally apply to those who possess such qualities, like *satyakāma*, for example, who was not aware of his strata in the society and was found suitable for spiritual fulfilment.[1] These *maṭhas* stood for the propagation and realization of the Advaita Vedānta. There was hardly any scope for making a distinction between one caste or the other. Even though a *śūdra*, if you do good you become a *Brāhmin*.[2]

Another important contribution of renunciation as an institution is the formation of the *pariṣad* (group of the *saṁnyāsins*) for the guidance of mankind. The reason why only renunciants were allowed to form such a group becomes obvious in the light of our previous observations. Such persons are the renunciants to whom the reference is made in the *Taittirīya Upaniṣad* : "Then, if there is in you any doubt regarding any deeds, any doubt regarding any conduct, you should behave yourself in such matters, as the *Brāhmaṇas* there (who are) competent to judge, devoted (to good deeds), not led by other, not harsh, lovers of virtue would behave in such cases.[3] In *Manu* and *Parāśara*, the importance of the *pariṣad* has been equally emphasized.

Parāśara thinks that a *pariṣad* should ordinarily consist of a hundred wise *Brāhmaṇas* but at the time of crisis only one *Brāhmaṇa* who is wise can serve as a *pariṣad*.[4] One of the *smṛtis* thinks that the opinion of such a wise person is as good as the

1. *paramahaṁsa-pārivrājyam pratipādya bhikṣācaryaṁ caranti bhikṣārtham caraṇam bhikṣācaryam caranti tyaktvā smārtaṁ liṅgaṁ kevalam āśrama-mātraśaraṇānām jīvanasādhanam pārivrājya vyānjabam. Śaṁkar. Bṛ. Up.* III.5.1.

2. *ebhistu karmabhir devīśubhair ācaritais tathā śūdro brāhmaṇatām yāti vaiśyaḥ kṣatriyatām vrajet.*

Quoted by S. Radhakrishnan, *Religion and Society*, p. 131.

3. *atha yadi te karmavicikitsā vā vṛtta vicikitsā vā syāt ye tatra brāhmaṇās sammarśinaḥ yuktā āyuktāḥ arukṣā dharmakāmās syuḥ yathā te tatra varteran tathā tatra vartethāḥ. Tai. Up.* I.77.4.

4. *munīnām ātmavidyānām dvijānām yajñayājinām*
vedavrateṣu snātānām eko'pi pariṣad bhavet. Parāśara, viii. 3.

authority of the Veda.[1] S. Radhakrishnan remarks: "Only those who are disciplined, compassionate to all living beings, learned in the Vedas and methods of logical inference, practical-minded (*deśakālavibhāgajñāḥ*) and of stainless character, have the power to legislate for the community."[2] Śaṁkara in his *bhāṣya* on the *Bṛhadāraṇyaka* remarks :

> It is therefore that in coming to a decision on a subtle point of *dharma*, it is desirable to have a *pariṣad* working and especially distinguished person (he means *saṁnyāsins*) is wanted (to give a lead) as stated in the rule, a *pariṣad* should consist of not less than ten persons or of three or of one (specially distinguished).[3]

Aṅgirasa confirms the same standpoint that a single person who is the best among ascetics, possessing knowledge of the Self may form a *pariṣad* and declare what a proper rule is on a point of doubt.[4]

A person who has been regarded as qualified to form a *pariṣad* is a person of utmost self-purification, without attachment to the fruits of his actions. He is an instrument for the cosmic purpose. Such a person has also been referred to a *Guru* (spiritual teacher) whose rank is equal to the rank of *Īśvara*.[5] The

1. *samayaścāpi sādhūnām pramāṇaṁ vedavad bhavet. dharmajñasamayaḥ pramāṇaṁ*. Quoted by S. Radhakrishnan, *Religion and Society*, p. 111.
2. *Ibid.*, p. 111.
3. For details, see Kane, *History of Dharmaśāstras*, II-II, 435-37.
4. *Yatīnām satyatapasā jñānavijñānacetasāṁ sirouratena snātānām ko'pi pariṣad bhavet.*

   Ibid., p. 969.
5. *ācāryavān puruṣo veda* (one who has a teacher knows.) *Ch. Up.* VI XIV.2. Śaṁkara thinks that only by help of a teacher who knows the Self, one can know the *sat*. See Radhakrishnan, *The Principal Upanisads*, p. 464. See Nancy W. Ross, *Three Ways of Asian Wisdom* (Mass. : A Clarion Book, 1969), p. 27.

   Cf. *Iśvaro gururātmetimūrtibhedabhāgine, vyomavad vyāptadehāya dakṣiṇamūrtaye namaḥ; yasya deve parābhaktiryathā deve tathā gurau.* *Śve. Up.* VI. 23.

   In the above passage devotion to God and teacher is shown as highly significant. Madhusūdan Sarasvatī, the author of *Advaitasiddhi*, shows great reverence to the *Avatāra* ideal and *Guru* ideal, See Ganganath Jha, trans., *Advaitasiddhi of Madhusūdana Sarasvatī in Indian Thought*. Vol. 10, (1917). R. D. Karmarkar, trans., *Vedāntakalpalatikā* (Poona : Bhandarkar Oriental Research Institute, 1962), verses 69 and 50. These verses assert the importance of teachers for the elimination of *avidyā*.

Saṁnyāsin here is the perfected man of self-realization who is free from all binding activities. The *avatāra* in Indian religious tradition is exemplary and is one who has self-realization but comes down to the world out of his own free will in order to guide and protect the world. Pure love based on *Jñāna* is the root of the service which the renunciants have inculcated in their method of the self-abnegation. The old and honoured traditions of *Guru* and *avatāra* still persist and derive their implications from the ideal of renunciation.

In the light of the above discussion, it may be pointed out that renunciation has taken precedence over almost all thought in India. In a sense, religious thought of India is renunciation orientated thought which found its fulfilment in every activity —individual, social and even political and economic. It is quite true that even in modern India, this tradition has its obvious impact. Yet it must be kept in mind that the tradition of renunciation is a very complex one. It is necessary to approach this subject with extreme care in order to avoid jumping to wrong conclusions pertaining to its nature.

CONCLUSION

In concluding this inquiry, I would like to make a few observations on some of the new perspectives from which the phenomenon of renunciation has been looked at in contemporary philosophical thought in India. Of all the systems of Indian philosophy, the *Vedānta* has the largest following in contemporary India. However, the exponents of this system are so different in their opinions that their views are not likely to find a common ground. But it is encouraging to note that there is an increasing tendency among them to view the Vedāntic philosophy as world-affirming, activistic and value-centred even though their approaches to the *raison d'etre* of the *Vedānta* are different. Our concern here is to indicate their opinions in the light of our undertaking and see the extent to which they could be helpful in the further understanding of this problem. There is, however, an obvious limitation here Some of these thinkers are not academic philosophers but spiritual leaders and mystics, making it difficult to understand precisely the general trends of their thought.

Some of these thinkers have contributed directly towards the ideal and discipline of renunciation on religious lines. Their writings and speeches are marked with fervent zeal and commitment to the socio-religious implications of renunciation. They have been *saṁnyāsins* of high order and their impact on Indian society and culture has been forceful and beneficial. It would be difficult to place them within either the new or old society, although their teachings and conduct have traditional orientations. They harnessed the traditional ideal of renunciation to the requirements and purposes of modern society. Renunciation for them served as a potential for this-worldly activism and cultural transformation. I do not see any reason for not accepting their contributions to the society on the model of renunciation. Men with their spiritual concerns might be supposed to manifest no interest in mundane activities. Yet far from this, these *saṁnyāsins* succeeded in building organizations and religious institutions which played a very vital role in the modernization of India. Inspirations for such tasks came to them from renunciation and asceticism which they found equally efficacious for individual salvation as well as salvation of the people of which they were representatives.

Without entering into details of their contributions, I will briefly indicate some of the directions they provided to the further understanding of renunciation. They accepted *Saṁnyāsa* as an institution (*āśrama*) oriented towards religio-social activities. The task they set to examine and accomplish were social issues, interpersonal relations, growth of the individual personality and creativity, a sense of unity, self-esteem and the cultivation and preservation of a unique sense of identity in terms of Indian values and meanings. The most striking feature of these architects of modern India was their resuscitation of the style of a *saṁnyāsin* who was not stranger to his own people. They had nothing to fear from him and he had nothing to take from them. Yet his status was irreconcilable with any kind of escapism or isolationism. His attitude is not of that of a simple spectator watching a show. He participates in the human drama with a personal detachment. To the extent he is attached, to that extent he is precluded from participation. Renunciation, for them was a renunciation of attachment in the interest of efficient and genuine participation. In a sense, renunciation for them was a disinterested interestedness. In the light of this it is easy to see why Vivekānanda, Swāmī Rāma Tīrtha, and Mahātmā Gāndhī were such successful innovators universally acceptable to India. They all fought against 'isolated individualism' and took renunciation as a guiding principle in opposing such a misconstrued notion. This strong sense of purpose based on the 'ascetic' ideal generated an atmosphere of hopefulness and strength which served to a considerable extent to create a nationwide revival. The life of activism, thus derived, became the expression of the spiritual order which took precedence over all petty considerations. This is only an interest of a higher order, but is interest any way. In the contemporary Indian philosophical context, I would call it the institutional theory of renunciation, supported largely and predominantly by the Vedāntic ideal as discussed in previous chapters.

Renunciation in its philosophical setting was strengthened by some of the modern philosophers in terms of Self-knowledge (*ātma-jñāna*), a deeper insight into one's own Self through the realization of the Supreme Spirit of eternal consciousness. The thinkers of the institutional type look into philosophy from the religio-social perspective but for the philosophers of this category, religion and social philosophy must stimulate the philosophical spirit. But it must be remembered, however, that despite the differences in their approaches, the ideal for both of them is the same, namely, a state of absolute peace (*śāntiṁ nirvāṇaparamāṁ*), infinite bliss (*sukhamātyantikaṁ*), complete equanimity (*nirdoṣam samam*), undisturbed intellect (*sthira-buddhirasammūḍhā*), Self-control (*antaḥ-nirodha*), fearlessness (*abhaya*). These states are desired here and now and not after death, here in this life while moving and doing actions (*ihaiva brahmaiva san brahma apyeti na śarirapātāduttarakālam*). It is the reason why philosophy in India was never hampered by religious thought. They served the cause in joint partnership and stood for the inculcation of the spirit of renunciation either aiming at Self-knowledge or God-realization.

It should be carefully noted here that renunciation has a very positive value whether it aims at Self-Knowledge (*ātma jñāna*) or God-realization (*brahma-saṁsparśam*). From the former standpoint, renunciation speaks to us of an experience which coincides with Reality, i.e. *Brahman*. In this sense, it unfolds itself along with the proper understanding of the structure of consciousness. J.G. Arapura regards it as the further extension of *jñāna* or consciousness which is all-inclusive and eternally present. To apply it here, one can deduce that differences in philosophies, and even philosophical interpretations are coordinated with the differences in the understanding of consciousness. It should then appear that the first task to do is to understand consciousness. In respect of the problem of consciousness, Advaita Vedānta provides a clear unitary perspective. The doctrine of renunciation, therefore, so far as it is also linked with the proper understanding of the world, must depend totally on the philosophy of consciousness. Only in this way, I regard it as a total way of life in Advaita Vedānta. Unlike asceticism, pure and simple, it is not by any means unrelated to thought.

Rather it becomes even an instrument or device of thought. It is constantly fed and sustained by the understanding of the nature of consciousness. This is unique to *Vedānta*. Renunciation, therefore, as an adjunct to thought does not either deny the world or doubt the world but simply modifies or radically changes our view of the world which is in 'existence'. But our interest is radically transformed in process of bringing the world with reference to what it is and not what it appears to be. In other words, a *saṁnyāsin* who is *brahmasaṁstha* abandons the naive attitude towards the world as a given reality independently of *Brahman* and in doing so he does not abandon the world.

There is no question of shifting the world from being something to being nothing as it is impossible even according to the Vedāntic metaphysics. What is to be shifted is the attitude regarding the world and all the activities associated with it. This means that man is involved with the world even before the dawn of *jñāna* and after the dawn of it but the way he was involved and is involved is different. In the state of *ajñāna* his involvement reflected a sense of "I-ness" (*ahaṁkāra*). In the state of *jñāna*, his involvement is meaningless in the sense that his "I-ness" is meaningless. The realization that *ahaṁkāra* is meaningless adds a full dimension of meaning to it which it never lacked but appeared to have been forgotten because of the *vāsanās* and *ajñāna*. With the fall of "I-ness", his involvement with the world on the basis of "I-ness" also falls to the ground but it does not remain in nothingness. The whole process is simultaneously attendant on the realization of Reality which transforms the nature of man to such an extent that it can be regarded as his re-birth. It is this relentless search of meaning that the *advaitins* try to discover through renunciation which has been shown to be linked with Self-knowledge. Put simply, once *ahaṁkāra* is burnt to ashes by the fire of knowledge, it is simultaneously accompanied by a further extension of the consciousness within which man establishes his greater identity. With this positive awareness (if I am permitted to say so), the world serves as an arena for discharging free and unmotivated activity as there is nothing left (with the elimination of *ahaṁkāra*) outside to generate any motive or self-seeking activity. At this stage, the individual as well as the world is sanctified on the basis of its radical extension within the general scheme of Reality. What was so far artificial becomes spontaneous. This is perhaps a far greater gain than the loss of the so-called individuality. By disowning oneself, as Kālidāsa puts in his *Mālavikāgnimitra*, one owns the whole world.

The contemporary philosophy occupied with such problem reflects a tendency of thought which I call the philosophical theory of renunciation. It may be regarded to be theoretical understanding of renunciation though in the final analysis it cannot be distinguished from the institutional theory of renunciation. A coherent study of the one would inevitably imply the other and both of them are equally important for the understanding of the personal and social dimensions or renunciation. They are held as distinct only in a theoretical sense.

In the contemporary Indian philosophical thought on the subject of the world, B.G. Tilak has attracted a good deal of attention. Renunciation, for him, is not the renunciation of action but renunciation of the fruits of action which he regards as the central theme of the *Gītā*. He complains against Śaṁkara that the Advaita Vedānta explains away the life of the disinterested activism by assigning it a secondary status for the purification of mind (*citta-śuddhi*). The disinterested action, for Tilak, is itself sufficient for the realization of freedom (*mokṣa*). He interprets Śaṁkara as propounding a philosophy of non-action, or cessation from action on the part of the *jñānin* or *saṁnyāsin*. He forgets that Śaṁkara does not take action in an ordinary sense of the term. By non-performance of action or *karma-saṁnyāsa*, the *advaitins* only mean that the *Brahmavid* or *Brahmasaṁstha* acts but automatically or spontaneously without any strain or struggle, due to the realization of the cosmic consciousness outside of which nothing remains. He does not struggle to be virtuous but becomes virtuous by nature. Tilak overlooks the advaitins' distinction between the *vividiṣā-saṁnyāsa* (renunciation of the seeker) and *vidvat-saṁnyāsa* (renunciation of the enlightened), a distinction I have dwelt upon at length before. Śaṁkara would accept everything, Tilak says in favour of the *Karmayogin* at the former level but at the latter level, the actions that are being performed by the *saṁnyāsins* are not the actions which Tilak has in mind but still they are actions of the free individual. The desire for the non-performance of action, because all actions imply distractions, will be a bondage for the *advaitins*, no less than a desire for performance. Tilak applauds the ideal of *lokasaṁgraha* and thinks that Śaṁkara denies that ideal. Śaṁkara does not deny that ideal either at cosmic or acosmic level. At the cosmic level, it is accompanied by the *sāttvika karma* on the model of *Īśvara*. On the acosmic level which does not have any trace of desire (*saṁkalpa*), it is automatically accomplished. Tilak refuses to go beyond the *sāttvika karma*, which is the realm of ethics. For Śaṁkara ethics must be established on the metaphysical foundation which does not deny the former but simply enriches it. This aspect of the problem which has found explicit expression in the contemporary Indian thought is what I call the activistic theory of renunciation. This again is a part of the Vedāntic concept of renunciation but not the whole of it.

The framework of reference which this dissertation attempted to set forth requires a different perspective to look into the development and consequences of the phenomenon of renunciation. Renunciation has emerged not merely as a 'theory' or 'thinking in a vacuum' but as a religiophilosophical thought which gradually developed into a kind of institution with its implications for overall transformation of life.

In the view which has been presented here, one may say, that renunciation provides one of the possible ways to identify oneself with the Reality but not the only way as has been asserted by Advaita Vedānta. An equally tenable view is that men who live by renunciation are partially choosing a different world, and therefore do not fully belong to this world. One's identity with the Reality, which necessarily implies casting off of one's individuality, can be substituted by other sets of values which are differently derived and perhaps oriented to a different world-view. This type of thinking comes not only from outside the tradition but from the tradition itself. Acceptance or rejection of any position is governed to a large extent by the values one is willing to embrace and perhaps there is hardly any controversy over this question. In other words, men committed to different set of values, may not hold renunciation as a universally acceptable valid way. They might find stronger support for devotion, worship, action, mythology, belief in this world alone and so on. We are not denying the existence of such tendencies of thought. What we are denying is the possibility of any system of broader commitment which is not at the same time sustained and pervaded by an urgent inculcation of the spirit of renunciation. The outstanding example of this is to be found in India throughout its religio-philosophical development. It would be wrong to think that the *Vedānta* denied any positive ideal of life through renunciation. It simply provided a metaphysical urge for a radical extension of such an ideal.

This problem has been tackled, in its ultimate analysis, not in isolation of one's Self from the whole but also removing any opposition whatsoever between the two. This we have called the acosmic ideal of the *Vedānta* represented by the *vidvat-saṁnyāsa* (renunciation of the enlightened). But we have shown clearly that this ultimate ideal does not exist in a vacuum. It must be sustained by the cosmic ideal of renunciation represented by *vividiṣā-saṁnyāsa* (renunciation of the seeker) where God is the spiritual model for the *sādhaka*. Renunciation, therefore is a very complex phenomenon and shapes the destiny of man in the holistic view of life. It cannot be brushed aside as a life-negating principle which was consistently assailed and denied by the *advaitins*; the falsity of which Śaṁkara was realizing every moment, not excluding the moment in which he was engaged in all kinds of creativity. Scholars who have misunderstood and misinterpreted Śaṁkara are not only those who could show some patience in understanding the *Vedānta* but unfortunately even those who falsely think that they belong to the Vedāntic tradition. The main point of issue for these thinkers is Śaṁkara's denial of the compatability, between i.e. simultaneous presence of *jñāna* and *karma*. They have understood it and misunderstood it. By the term, 'action' Śaṁkara means artificial action, generating all kinds of egoism, and not spontaneous action or free action which does not bind the individual and also does not hinder the growth and advancement of the society. The action of the latter type is spiritual action sustained by *Jñāna* which we have found as equivalent to renunci ation (*saṁnyāsa*). The real problem for the *Advaitins* does not lie in acceptance or denial of action; it does not interest a philosopher to deny what common sense assumes. The advaitins' task is to provide an explanation which significantly lies in the transforming aspect of actions by *jñāna*. The same pattern of thought is equally true with regard to the world. Renunciation consists essentially in transforming the nature of man and the universe—a transformation whose accomplishment consists in manifesting or letting the true nature of them emerge to the surface.

The central thrust of the present thesis, as has been shown, lies in a proper understanding of the meaning and scope of renunciation in Advaita Vedānta. Renunciation, is by no means a philosophy of pessimism, escapism or a formal and external type of asceticism. The whole objective of renunciation, its entire *raison d'etre*, is *jñāna* (saving knowledge) which again is not a dull quietism or isolationism but an enlightened attitude towards life, society and the world and, in fact, every activity in society and the world. If Advaita Vedānta attaches the highest importance to renunciation, it did so because of its conviction that the ideal of renunciation alone can sanctify human interests whether individual, social, ethical, religious or spiritual. Whenever, renunciation exhibited any exclusive otherworldly direction, anti-moralism, fatalism, individualism, predeterminism, and the like, the Vedānta tradition sharply reacted against those tendencies. The positive standard of the Vedānta tradition deeply and scrutinizingly thought over these life-negating attitudes in order to free society from disintegration and decay. The unbroken continuity of this tradition until today speaks for itself. If it stops short or fails to develop its true spirit, it is a serious crisis and needs close scrutiny not only into itself but the whole structure of life.

BIBLIOGRAPHY

Major Sources

The Upaniṣads

Gambhīrānanda, Swāmī, trans. and ed. *Eight Upaniṣads: With the Commentary by Śaṅkarācārya.* 2 Vols. Calcutta: Advaita Ashrama, 1957-58.

Jhā, G.N., trans. and ed. *The Chāndogya Upaniṣad* (A Treatise on Vedānta Philosophy Translated into English with the Commentary of Śaṁkara). With an Introduction and Index by Umesha Mishra. Poona: Oriental Book Agency, 1942.

Madhvananda, Swami, trans. *The Bṛhadāraṇyaka Upaniṣad* (With the Commentary of Śaṅkarācārya). Calcutta: Advaita Ashrama, 1965.

Radhakrishnan S, trans., and ed. *The Principal Upaniṣads.* With Introduction, Text and Notes. London : George Allen and Unwin Ltd. 1953. (In America: Humanities Press Inc. of New York).

The Bhagavad Gitā

Desai, Mahadeva, trans. *The Gospel of Selfless Action or the Gita According to Gandhi.* Translation of the original in Gujarati with an Additional Introduction and Commentary. 4th Impression. Ahmedabad: Navajivan Publishing House, 1956.

Radhakrishnan, S., trans. and ed. *The Bhagavadgītā.* With an Introductory Essay, Sanskrit Text, English Translation and Notes. London: George Allen and Unwin Ltd., 1948.

Sastri, A. Mahadeva, trans. *The Bhagvad-Gitā: With the Commentary of Sri Sankaracharya.* Madras: V. Ramaswamy Sastrulu and Sons, 1961.

Tilak, B. G. *Gita Rahasya.* Translated by S.S., Suthankar. 2nd edition. Poona: Lokamanya Tilak Mandir, 1965.

The Vedānta Sūtras

Bakre, M. S., ed. *Brahmasūtrabhāṣya with Ratnaprabhā, the Bhāmati and Nyāyanirṇaya*. Bombay: Nirnayasagara Press, 1934.

Radhakrishnan, S., trans. *The Brahmasūtra* (the Philosophy of Spiritual Life). With an Introduction and Note. London: George Allen and Unwin Ltd., 1960.

Thibaut, George, trans. *The Vedānta-sūtras with the Commentary of Sankaracarya*. Edited by F. Max Muller in the Sacred Books of the East, Vols XXXIV, XXXVIII. Oxford : Clarendon Press, 1890, 1896. (In India: Motilal Banarsidass, Delhi).

The Naiṣkarmyasiddhi

Alston, J. A., trans. *The Naiṣkarmyasiddhi of Śrī Sureśvara*. London: Shanti Sadan, 1959.

Agase, K. S., ed. *Sureśvara's Vārttika on Śaṅkara's Bṛhadāraṇyakopaniṣadabhāṣya*. Poona: Anandasrama Sanskrit Series, 1892-94.

Raghavachar, S. S., trans. *Śrī Sureśvara's Naiṣkarmyasiddhi*. Mysore: University of Mysore, 1965.

The Vivekacūḍāmaṇi

Madhvananda, Swami, trans. *Śaṅkarācārya's Vivekacūḍāmaṇi or Crest-Jewel of Discrimination*. Calcutta: Advaita Ashrama, 1921.

The Pañcadaśī

Shastri, H. P., tras. *Pañcadaśī: A Treatise on Advaita Metaphysics by Swāmi Vidyāraṇya*. London: Shanti Sadan, 1966.

The Jivan-Mukti-Viveka

Sastri, S. S. and T. R. S. Ayyangar, eds, and trans. *The Jivan-Mukti-Viveka or The Path of Liberation in this Life of Śrī Vidyāraṇya*. Madras: The Theosophical Publishing House, 1935.

The Upadeśasāhasri

Jagadanand, Swami, trans. *The Upadeśasāhasri of Śrī Śankaracharya*. Madras: Sri Ramakrishna Matha, 1961.

The Pañcapādikāvivaraṇa

Venkataramiah, D., trans. *The Pañcapādikāvivaraṇa of Padmapāda*. Gaekwad Oriental Series, Vol. 107. Baroda: Oriental Institute, 1948.

The Vedāntaparibhāṣā

Sastri, S. S. Suryanarayana, ed. and trans. *Vedāntaparibhāṣā by Dharmarāja Adhvarin*. Madras: The Adyar Library, 1942.

SOME MAJOR SECONDARY SOURCES

Arapura, J. G. *Religion as Anxiety and Tranquillity*. The Hague, Paris: Mouton, 1972.

,, *Radhakrishnan and Integral Experience*. New York: Asia Publishing House, 1966.

Barua, B. M. *A History of Pre-Buddhistic Indian Philosophy*, Delhi: Motilal Banarsidass, 1970. (First published by Calcutta University Press of Calcutta, 1921).

Basham, A. L. *History and Doctrines of Ajivakas*. London: Luzac and Co., 1951.

Bhattacharya., H., ed. *The Cultural Heritage of India*. 4 Vols. Calcutta: The Ramakrishna Mission, 1969.

Brahma, N. K. *Philosophy of Hindu Sadhana*. London: Kegan Paul, Trench, Trubner and Co. Ltd., 1932.

Bühler, Georg, *The Laws of Manu—Translated with Extracts from Seven Commentaries*. Edited by F. Max Muller, SBE. Vol. xxv. Oxford: The Clarendon Press, 1886.

Chakraborti, H. *Asceticism in Ancient India*. Calcutta: Punthi Pustak, 1973.

Dasgupta, S.N. *Hindu Mysticism*. New York: Federick Udgar Publishing Co., 1971.

,, *History of Indian Philosophy*. 4 Vols. Cambridge: Cambridge University Press, 1922-55.

,, *Philosophical Essays*. Calcutta: University of Calcutta, 1941.

Deussen, Paul. *The Philosophy of the Upanisads*. Translated by A. S. Geden. New York: Dover Publications, 1968.

,, *The System of Vedānta*. Translated by Charles Johnston. Delhi: Motilal Banarsidass, 1972.

Deutsch, E. *A Source Book of Advaita Vedānta.* Honolulu: The University Press of Hawaii, 1971.

Dubois, A. *Hindu Manners, Customs and Ceremonies.* Oxford: The Clarendon Press, 1906.

Dutt, S. *Buddhist Monks and Monasteries in India.* London: George Allen and Unwin Ltd., 1962.

„ *Early Buddhist Monachism.* Bombay: Asia Publishing House, 1960.

Eliade, M. *Yoga: Immortality and Freedom.* Translated by Willard R. Trask. Princeton: Princeton University Press, 1970.

Farquhar, J. N. and H. D. Griswald. *The Religious Quest of India.* London: Oxford University Press, 1922.

Ghurye, G. S. *Indian Sadhus.* Bombay: Popular Prakashan, 1964.

Hiriyanna, M. *Outlines of Indian Philosophy* London: George Allen and Unwin Ltd., 1968.

„ ed. and trans. *Vedanta-Sara by Sadananda : A Work on Vedanta Philosophy.* Poona: Oriental Book Agency, 1929.

„ trans. *Śaṁkarācārya's Kenopaniṣadbhāṣya.* Srirangam, 1915.

Iyer, M. K. V. *Advaita Vedanta According to Śaṁkara.* New York: Asia Publishing House, 1964.

Jha, G. N. trans. *Yoga Darsana: The Sutras of Patanjali With the Bhāṣya of Vyāsa.* Bombay: R. T Talya for Bombay Theosophical Publication Fund, 1907.

Kale, M. R., trans. *The Niti and Vairagya Sataka of Bhartrihari.* Delhi: Motilal Banarsidass, 1971.

Kane, P. V. *History of Dharmasastra.* 4 Vols. Poona: Bhandarkar Oriental Research Institute, 1930-53.

Karmarkar, R. D. trans. *Vedāntakalpalatikā.* Poona: Bhandarkar Oriental Research Institute, 1962.

Keith, A. B. *The Religion and Philosophy of the Veda and Upaniṣads.* 2 Vols. Delhi: Motilal Banarsidass, 1970.

Krishna Warrier, A. G. *The Concept of Mukti in Advaita Vedanta.* Madras: University of Madras, 1961.

Majumdar, R. C. and others. *An Advanced History of India.* London: George Allen and Unwin Ltd., 1963.

Mahadevan, T. M. P. *The Philosophy of Advaita.* Foreword by S. Radhakrishnan. Madras: Ganesh and Co., 1969.

Mol, Hans. *Sacralization of Identity*, Manuscript. Canada: McMaster University, 1974.

Motawani, K. *Manu Dharma Sastra*. Madras: Ganesh and Co., 1958.

Murti, T. R. V. *The Central Philosophy of Buddhism*. London: George Allen and Unwin Ltd., 1960.

Murty, K. S., ed. *Readings in Indian History, Philosophy and Politics*. London: George Allen and Unwin Ltd., 1967.

,, *The Indian Spirit*. Waltair: Andhra University Press, 1965.

Nikhilananda, Swami, trans. *Self-Knowledge; An English Translation of Śaṁkarāchārya's Ātmabodha*. Madras: Sri Ramakrishna Math, 1947.

,, ed. and trans. *The Upanisads*. New York: Harper and Row, 1964.

Oman, J. G. *The Mystics, Ascetics and Saints of India*. Calcutta: Punthi Pustak, 1905.

Otto, R. *Mysticism East and West*. Translated by E. L. Bracey and R. C. Payne. New York: Collier Books, 1962.

Prabhu, P. H. *Hindu Social Organization*. Bombay: Popular Prakashan, 1963.

Radhakrishnan, S. *The Hindu View of Life*. London: George Allen and Unwin Ltd., 1927.

,, *Indian Philosophy*. 2 Vols. New York: The Macmillan Co. Ltd., London: George Allen and Unwin Ltd., 1923 and 1927.

,, *Religion and Society*. London: George Allen and Unwin Ltd., 1969.

,, *East and West in Religion*. London: George Allen and Unwin Ltd., 1949.

Radhakrishnan, S. and Charles A. Moore, eds. *A Source Book in Indian Philosophy*. Princeton: Princeton University Press, 1957.

Rao, K. S. R. *Advaita as a Philosophy and Religion*, Prasaranga: University of Mysore, 1969.

Ranade, R. D. *A Constructive Survey of Upanisadic Philosophy*. Poona: Oriental Book Agency, 1926.

Rudolph, L. I. R. and Susanne H. Rudolph. *The Modernity of Tradition*. Chicago: The University of Chicago Press, 1967.

Samartha, S. J. *The Hindu View of History, Classical and Modern.* Bangalore, 1950.

Sastri, S. S. *The Life and Teachings of Sankaracharya.* Madras: G.A. Natesan and Co. n.d.

Sastri, S.S.S. and R.C. Kunhan, eds. and trans. *The Bhamati of Vacaspati: on Samkara's Brahmasutrabhasya.* Adyar: The Theosophical Publishing House, 1933.

Singer, M. *Traditional India: Structure and Change.* Philadelphia: American Folklore Society, 1959.

Singh, R.P. *The Vedānta of Śaṁkara: A Metaphysics of Value.* Jaipur: Bharat Printing House, 1949.

Sivaraman, K. *Saivism in Philosophical Perspective.* Delhi: Motilal Banarsidass, 1973.

Sprung, M., ed. *Two Truths in Buddhism and Vedānta.* Dordrecht, Holland : Reidel, 1973.

Srinivasa, M. N. *Social Change in Modern India.* Berkeley and Los Angeles : University of California Press, 1969.

Tagore, R. N. *The Religion of Man.* London : George Allen and Unwin Ltd., 1931.

Tatia, N. *Studies in Jain Philosophy.* Benares : Jain Cultural Research Society, 1951.

Tylor, S. A. *India : An Anthropological Perspective,* California : Goodyear Publishing Co., 1973.

Visveswarananda, Swami, ed. *Brahma-sūtras*, Mayavati, Almora: Advaita Ashrama, 1948.

Weber, M. The *Religion of India : The Sociology of Hinduism and Buddhism.* Translated and edited by H. H. Gerth and D. Martindale, Illinois : Glencoe, 1958.

Zimmer, H. *Philosophies of India.* Edited by Joseph Campbell. Princeton : Princeton University Press, 1969.

Secondary Sources

Acharya, Anand. *Brahmadarśanam, an Introduction to the Study of Hindu Philosophy.* New York : The Macmillan Co., 1917.

Aurobindo, Śri. *Foundations of Indian Culture.* Pondichery : Aurobindo Ashrama, 1953.

Banerjee, S. C. *Dharma-sūtras : A Study in their Origin and Development.* Calcutta : Punhit Pustak, 1962.

Bhandarkar, D. R. *Some Aspects of Ancient Indian Culture.* Bombay, 1940.

Bhandarkar, R. G. *Vaisnavism, Śaivism and Minor Religious Sects.* Varanasi : Indological Book House, 1965.

Bhattacharya, A. S. *Studies in Post-Śankara Dialectics.* Calcutta : University of Calcutta, 1936.

Brown, W. N. *Man in the Universe.* Berkeley and Los Angeles : University of California Press, 1966.

Carstairs, M. *The Twice Born : A Study of a Community of High Caste Hindus.* London : George Allen and Unwin Ltd., 1957.

Dasgupta, S. N. *Indian Idealism.* Cambridge : The University Press, 1933.

Das, S. K. *A Study of Vedānta.* Calcutta: University of Calcutta, 1937.

Devaraja, N. K. *The Mind and Spirit of India.* Delhi : Motilal Banarsidass, 1967.

Durkheim, E. *The Elementary Forms of the Religious Life.* Translated from the French by Joseph Ward Swain. New York : The Free Press, 1967.

Farquhar, J. N. *An Outline of the Religious Literature of India.* London : Oxford University Press, 1920.

Gokhale, B. G. *Indian Thought Through the Ages : A Study of Some Dominant Concepts.* Bombay, 1961.

Gunaratne, U. F. *The Significance of the Four Noble Truths.* Kandy : B. P. S., 1868.

Hopkins, E. W. *Religion of India.* Boston, London : Ginn and Co. Publishers, 1895.

„ *Ethics of India.* New Haven : Yale University Press, 1924.

Jacobi, H., trans. *Jain Sutras.* Edited by F. Max Muller, SBE, Vol. XXII. Oxford : The Clarendon Press, 1884.

Keith, A. B. *History of Sanskrit Literature.* Delhi : Asia Publishing House, 1962.

Kinjewadekar, R. C. S., ed. *Śrīman Mahābhārata.* Poona : Chitrasala Press, 1932.

Mackenzie, J. L. *The Roman Catholic Church.* New York : Holt, Rinehart and Winston, 1969.

Maitra, S. K. *The Ethics of the Hindus*. Calcutta : University of Calcutta, 1925.

Metcalf, T. R. *Modern India : An Interpretative Anthology*. London : The Macmillan Co., 1971.

Mishra, V. *Hinduism and Economic Growth*. Bombay : Oxford University Press, 1962.

Raju, P. T. *Idealistic Thought of India*. Cambridge : Harvard University Press, 1953.

Rhys Davids, T. W. *Buddhist India*. New York : G. P. Putnam's Sons, 1903.

Roosevelt, E. *India and the Awakening East*. New York : Harper and Brothers, 1953.

Roy, M. N. *New Orientations*. Calcutta : Renaissance Publishers, n.d.

,, *Beyond Communism*. Calcutta : Renaissance Publishers, n.d.

Sastrigal, K. C. and V. H. Sastri, eds. *Śrīmadvālmīkirāmāyaṇa*. Mylapore, Madras : The M. L. J. Press, 1958.

Schweitzer, A. *Indian Thought and its Development*. Translated by Mrs. Charles E. B. Russell. Bombay, 1960.

Weber, M. *The Protestant Ethic and the Spirit of Capitalism*. Translated by T. Parsons. New York, 1958.

Winternitz, M. *History of Indian Literature*. Calcutta : University of Calcutta, 1963.

Woods. J. H., trans. *The Yoga System of Patanjali or the Ancient Hindu Doctrine of Concentration of Mind*. Mass : Harvard Oriental Series, 1927.

PERIODICALS

Arapura, J. G., "The Upside Down Tree of the Bhagavad Gītā, Ch. VI". *Numena*, XXCII (Forthcoming April, 1975).

Bodhananda, "Renunciation, *Vedanta Magazine*', II (1906-07), 84-92.

Brahma, N. K., "Vedantic Intuition", *Proceedings of Indian Philosophical Congress*, I (1925), 166-173.

Bühler, G., "The Barabar and Nagarjuna Hill Cave Inscriptions of Asoka and Dasaratha", *The Indian Antiquary*, XX (1901), 362.

Chaitanya, P , "Renunciation as an Ideal of Life", *Vedanta Kesari*, xv (1928-29), 416-423.

Datta, D. M., "Inward and Outward Advaita Vedanta". *The Philosophical Quarterly*, xxx (1957), 165-72.

Deussen, Paul, "The Philosophy of the Vedanta in its relation to the Occidental Metaphysics", *Journal of the Royal Asiatic Society of Great Britain and Ireland*, xiii (1890-94), 330-40.

Duetsch, E., "The Self in Advaita Vedānta", *Indian Philosophical Quarterly*, vi-i (1966), 5-21.

Hiriyanna, M., 'The Ethics of Advaita", *Vedanta Kesari*, xxix (1942-43), 109-113.

Ingalls, D. H. H., "Śaṁkara on the Question : Whose is Avidyā ?", *Philosophy East and West*, iii (1953), 69-72.

,, "Cynics and Pāśupatas : The Seeking of Dishonour", *Harvard Theological Review*, lv (1952), 239-45.

Jagadiswarananda, "Advaita and Sannyasa" *Quarterly Journal of the Mythic Society*, i (1906), 54.

Mahadevan. T. M. P., "The Metaphysics of Sankara", *Philosophy East and West*, iii, No. 4 (1954), 359-64.

,, "Can There be Ethics Without Metaphysics", *Indian Philosophical Proceedings*, (1952), 284-297.

Modi, P. M., "Development of the Systems of Ashrama", *Proceedings and Transactions of the Seventh All India Oriental Conference*, (Baroda, 1935), 377-389.

Murti, T. R. V., "Rational Basis of Advaitism", *Philosophical Quarterly*, vi (1930), 57-81.

,, "The Two Definitions of Brahman in Advaita", *K. C. Bhattacharya Memorial Volume* (Amalner, 1958), 89-105.

Raghavan, V., "Some Leading Ideas of Hindu Thought", *The Vedanta Kesari*, (Feb., 1955), 109-121.

Sharma, H. D., "History of Brahmanical Asceticism", *Poona Orientalist*, iii, No. 4 (1939), 44-57.

Singer, M., Cultural Values in India's Economic Development", *The Annals of American Academy of Political and Social Sciences*, 305 (1956), 81-91.

,, "Religious and Social Change in India : The Max Weber's Thesis, Phase Three", *Economic Development and Cultural Change*, xiv (1965-66), 497-505.

Singer, M., "Review of Max Weber's Religion of India", *American Anthropology*, LXIII (1961), 85-94.

Skorpen, E. "The Philosophy of Renunciation East and West", *Philosophy East and West*. (July, 1971), pp. 284-295.

Tambiah, S. J., "Buddhism and This-Worldly Activity", *Modern Asian Studies*, VIII-1 (1973), 16-28.

Toynbee, A. J., "The Desert Hermits", *Horizon*, XII-2 (Spring, 1970), 26-39.

Winternitz, M., "Ascetic Literature in Ancient India", *Calcutta University Review* (October, 1923), pp. 3-10.

INDEX